D1492567

SWANSEA LIBRARIES
WITHDRAWN
6000325102

THE EASY FASTING
5:2 DIET
COOKBOOK

THE EASY FASTING
5:2 DIET
COOKBOOK

Make fast days feel like feast days, with 130 delicious recipes

PENNY DOYLE

LORENZ BOOKS

This edition is published by Lorenz Books,
an imprint of Anness Publishing Ltd,
108 Great Russell Street, London WC1B 3NA;
info@anness.com   twitter: @Anness_Books
www.lorenzbooks.com; www.annesspublishing.com

If you like the images in this book and would
like to investigate using them for publishing,
promotions or advertising, please visit our website
www.practicalpictures.com for more information.

© Anness Publishing Ltd 2018

All rights reserved. No part of this publication may be
reproduced, stored in a retrieval system, or transmitted in
any way or by any means, electronic, mechanical,
photocopying, recording or otherwise, without the prior
written permission of the copyright holder.

A CIP catalogue record for this book is available from
the British Library.

Publisher: Joanna Lorenz
Executive Editor: Joanne Rippin
Designer: Adelle Mahoney

PUBLISHER'S NOTE
Although the advice and information in this book are
believed to be accurate and true at the time of going to
press, neither the author nor the publishers can accept
any legal responsibility or liability for any errors or
omissions that may have been made nor for any
inaccuracies nor for any loss, harm or injury that comes
about from following instructions or advice in this book.
Both the author and publisher strongly recommend that
a doctor or other healthcare professional is consulted
before embarking on major dietary changes.

COOK'S NOTES
Bracketed terms are intended for American readers.
For all recipes, quantities are given in both metric and
imperial measures and, where appropriate, in
standard cups and spoons. Follow one set of
measures, but not a mixture, because they are not
interchangeable.

Standard spoon and cup measures are level.
1 tsp = 5ml, 1 tbsp = 15ml, 1 cup = 250ml/8fl oz.
Australian standard tablespoons are 20ml. Australian
readers should use 3 tsp in place of 1 tbsp for
measuring small quantities. American pints are
16fl oz/2 cups. American readers should use 20fl oz/
2.5 cups in place of 1 pint when measuring liquids.

Electric oven temperatures in this book are for
conventional ovens. When using a fan oven, the
temperature will probably need to be reduced by
about 10–20°C/20–40°F. Since ovens vary, you
should check with your manufacturer's instruction
book for guidance.

The nutritional analysis given for each recipe is
calculated per portion (i.e. serving or item), unless
otherwise stated. If the recipe gives a range, such as
Serves 4–6, then the nutritional analysis will be for
the smaller portion size, ie 6 servings. The analysis
does not include optional ingredients, such as salt
added to taste.

Medium (US large) eggs are used unless
otherwise stated.

CITY AND COUNTY OF SWANSEA LIBRARIES	
6000325102	
Askews & Holts	21-Jun-2018
641.563	£10.00
SK	

CONTENTS

INTRODUCTION

Intermittent fasting, when food intake is considerably reduced for part of the week, is becoming increasingly popular with those wanting to lose weight without having to measure their calorie intake every day.

There are a number of ways to approach intermittent fasting: 2 days out of 7 (5:2 dieting) is the most well-known, but some people follow a 4:3 plan, or even alternate days. Each plan is proving to be particularly appealing to people who want to reduce abdominal spread and protect against the risk of diseases. Followers are often those who love cooking and sharing meals, and are aware of the health benefits and improved energy levels of eating properly.

The basic concept of intermittent fasting is that women restrict their daily energy intake to 500 calories a day, and men to 600 calories a day, for two or more days each week, leaving you free to consume a healthy, balanced diet for the remaining days. A number of plans and books are available: *The Every Other Day Diet* by nutritionist Dr Krista Varaday and Bill Gottlieb advocates a 4:3 regimen, while Dr James Johnson's *Alternate Day Diet* recommends fasting every other day. Dr Michelle Harvie and Professor Tony Howell's book *The 2 Day Diet*, and Michael Mosley and Mimi Spencer's *The Fast Diet*, both offer compelling new research in their recommendation of a 5:2 fasting diet plan.

These fasting regimes have created a need for tightly calorie controlled recipes that offer healthy, balanced dishes, which satisfy the appetite and make fasting days easier to manage. This book features all kinds of light meals, snacks and main courses to help you through those challenging fasting days. Containing a range of recipes with a total

calorie count of between 50 and 500, the book will help you plan your intake depending on how you wish to structure the day. For instance you may choose to eat a 100-calorie breakfast and a 300-calorie supper, and use 100 calories for hot drinks throughout the day, or fast for most of the day with only 50 calories of snacks and hot drinks but then eat a much larger 450-calorie supper. Recipes come with full nutritional breakdowns, with ideas for tweaking the calorie counts, depending on your totals. There is also advice for men, on adjusting the day to 600 calories.

The key to fasting recipes is that they contain adequate protein, lower glycaemic index (GI) carbohydrates, and great flavours, all of which will help maintain energy levels. Pleasingly, this also includes moderate amounts of salt, which is explained later.

As a registered dietitian, I have a wealth of experience and success in helping individuals comply with and get results from weight-reducing diets, and am aware of how important it is to include the right foods to help curb hunger pangs. I also believe that in following any diet there is an element of 'no pain, no gain'. In a world of constantly available food, it won't always be easy to keep up commitment levels, but many people are achieving impressive results with intermittent fasting diets, including reduced waistlines, better mobility, and lowered cholesterol and blood pressure. With some forward planning and determination, and with this thoughtfully-planned collection of tempting recipes, you should be able to achieve a slimmer, healthier and happier lifestyle.

Penny Doyle

NUTRITION AND MODERN EATING PATTERNS

Recent research on the causes of modern obesity has led us to reassess how our bodies are biologically wired for a very different society to the one many of us live in. Our Paleolithic ancestors developed appetites and metabolisms that thrived on periods of feast and famine, the opposite type of environment from today's access to plentiful food. It is now believed that times of food scarcity helped our bodies to become stronger, adapting to the challenges of energy storage, and processing food more efficiently when it was available.

An obesogenic environment
Modern eating habits, 'grazing', convenience foods, lower activity levels and ease of transport, have all contributed to creating very different circumstances, now referred to as the obesogenic environment, which actually predisposes us to gain weight.

Fast food, a relentless supply of snacks, and eating on the move means that people eat more high-fat, high-sugar foods on a daily basis. Each day we experience consumer pressure to buy chocolate, crisps (US potato chips), pastries and sweets, on the street, at work, at school, even at sporting venues and petrol stations, all of it unnecessary 'fuel' as we continue on sedentary car journeys. By stark comparison, our Paleolithic ancestors would have had to work hard and expend energy to achieve every aspect of their lives: hunting and foraging for food, building shelter, and fighting or moving on to maintain their safety.

Our biological makeup means that our bodies, programmed at a time when food was often scarce, are compelled to guard against starvation, which means we may feel the desire to eat simply because food is there, not because we need it. Hunger, counter-intuitively, is a poor indicator of our nutritional needs, desensitised as it is by regular access to food and drink. Understanding this and adopting a 'mind over matter' approach to dieting and weight management is critical to losing and maintaining weight loss on a fasting regime.

The benefits of weight reduction
Being overweight is associated with a higher risk of developing a number of chronic modern diseases, including Type 2 diabetes, heart disease, high blood pressure and stroke, asthma, cancer, reproductive problems and arthritis, among others. The good news is that even a loss of 5% body weight, 3kg/7lbs for a 60kg/9.5 stone woman, or 3.5kg/8lbs for a 70kg/11 stone man, could significantly reduce these risks, particularly for heart disease, diabetes and some cancers.

A healthy diet
Intermittent fasting diets recommend following a healthy diet for most of the time, so for 5 out of 7 days consuming energy (calories)

◀ Before mechanization, grinding grains to make them edible took a huge amount of human energy.

levels of around 2,000 calories a day for women and 2,500 for men. This diet should include moderate fat intake, predominantly from healthier polyunsaturated fats including oily fish, nuts and seeds, but less from saturated animal sources such as meat, cheese and butter. Protein should be derived from a range of plant and animal sources for example meat, fish, eggs, pulses, nuts and grains. A healthy diet should also include a regular intake of slowly-absorbed, high fibre carbohydrates from cereals, brown rice and wholegrain bread, and plenty of fibre from fruit and vegetables.

For the remaining 2 or more fasting days in a week, energy intake should be restricted to less than a third of a person's average requirement (usually around 500 calories for women and 600 for men). This reduction in calorie intake has the effect of forcing the body to mobilize fat stores, in the kind of emergency reaction our bodies were designed for, resulting in weight loss.

▲ Protein in a healthy diet should be from a range of sources, while fresh vegetables and fruit should make up a third of your total daily intake of food.

Nutrition basics

Knowing a little bit about basic nutrition is useful for understanding how our bodies use fuel, and why weight might change. Food provides us with three main macronutrients, protein, carbohydrates and fats, as well as many vitamin and mineral micronutrients. Although technically not a nutrient, as it isn't absorbed, we also need fibre from fruits, vegetables and grains for effective digestion and bowel health.

Proteins, sourced mainly from meat, fish, eggs, nuts, pulses, and soya products, are a key component of body tissues, and play many important physiological roles within the blood, hormones and immune system. Contrary to the theories of high-protein diets, as adults we only need limited amounts of protein, and too much is a definite contributor to obesity.

▲ Low GI carbohydrates, when combined with protein like nuts or tofu, leave us feeling satisfied for longer.

Carbohydrates, from cereals, rice, pasta and bread, are broken down by the body into usable glucose, and are essential for physical movement and brain activity. Glucose is the primary fuel used by the brain, which is why we can go dizzy and faint sometimes when food intake is limited. However, carbohydrate foods can leave you hungrier if absorbed too quickly, which is why we are encouraged to eat more slowly-digested, lower glycemic index (GI) foods such as whole grains, seeds, root vegetables and oats, in lieu of higher GI white bread and rice, pasta, potatoes and refined cereals. Low GI carbohydrates, when combined with suitable protein, vegetables and some fats or oils, will leave you feeling full for longer and help limit your food intake to healthy amounts.

Energy balance
All the energy that our bodies need for maintenance of Basal Metabolic Rate (BMR), and external work such as movement, comes from macronutrients, but in differing amounts. Significantly, fat in food provides over twice as much energy per gram (9 calories), compared to protein or carbohydrate (both 4 calories per gram), which is why many weight-reducing diets focus on lowering fat intake.

While this is a sound theory, recent research suggests that very low-fat diets may start depleting vital protein stores instead of body fat. Another drawback is that low-fat diets are difficult to maintain, hence the ongoing interest in diets that may prove to be more sustainable, such as intermittent fasting.

Fasting facts
Periods without food have been a part of human society since Paleolithic times, when our ancestors foraged for berries, roots and leaves. In effect this was an enforced fast, broken when the community had a successful hunt or found a plentiful supply of ripe fruits or grains. The ancient Greeks believed fasting to be an important part of recovery after an illness, and it was perhaps the Egyptians that first linked it to religious observance. Voluntary fasting continued as major religions developed, and Christians, Muslims, Sikhs, Jews and Buddhists encouraged it to heighten levels of consciousness, spirituality and discipline. Whatever reason a controlled fast is undertaken, it is important to understand what kind of physical changes are happening to the body while it takes place.

How the body reacts
When we fast there are clever physiological changes going on as the body tries to protect itself for as long as possible. Energy for BMR, which remains at around 1 calorie per minute for men, and 0.8 calories per minute for women, must be maintained, but falls slightly during fasting to help conserve stores. At first,

when food is limited, the body will utilize muscle and liver carbohydrate stores (glycogen), but these run out within hours when the body has to switch to fat or protein stores for energy. So long as there is some fat or oil in the diet, the body will use fat stores, which is better for health and weight loss. However if there is no fat in the diet at all, our bodies will be forced to use body tissue and muscle for vital energy, which can be dangerous and life threatening.

Fortunately nothing so drastic as this will occur in intermittent fasting diets, as the famine period is rarely longer than 24 hours, and the diet includes a small proportion of healthy fats, but the ongoing food restriction will enable fat stores to be mobilized resulting in healthy weight loss. As fat stores are mobilized the body will produce more water and 'ketones' in the blood, which are a safe by-product of fat breakdown but may produce distinct smelling breath.

On very low-carbohydrate, high-protein diets the body's initiation of 'ketosis' is almost aspirational, but it is certainly not necessary for weight loss and should be avoided. Use of fat stores also causes loss of electrolytes, including some sodium (salt), which is why you should include some salt in your food on fasting days

The preservation of muscle and body protein in intermittent dieting is clearly good from the point of view of overall health, but also for maintaining a lighter weight, as resting muscle uses more calories than body fat, so a leaner person will expend more calories doing nothing than a fatter person.

Improved insulin function
We know that there is improved function of the hormone insulin after fasting. Insulin is most commonly known for helping to control blood sugar levels, but is also key to the metabolism of protein and fat, and will contribute to obesity if blood levels are consistently high. After fasting, the body reduces insulin production, which helps slow the storage of body fat.

Feel good factors
Natural neurotransmitters 'endorphins' are released into the blood when food is restricted, which helps to raise alertness and create a feeling of well-being, similar to that experienced during exercise or sexual activity. These feelings will also help intermittent fasting dieters stick to their regimens and contribute to success.

Advocates of alternate day fasting believe that the 'skinny gene' SIRT1 is activated when body cells are fasted, and that this boosts the metabolism and limits storage of fat, but definitive research so far is limited.

▼ Steamed greens, spiced up with chilli, are high in flavour but low in calories.

POTENTIAL HEALTH BENEFITS FROM FASTING

Intermittent fasting is popular not just because of the weight loss, but also because of the growing evidence of wider health benefits.

Reduced cancer risk
Research by Dr Michelle Harvie and Professor Tony Howell has indicated some reduction in the risk of breast cancer, related to obesity, for which they developed the 2 Day Diet. The theory is that fasting and deprivation of nutrients seems beneficial at a cellular level by a biological method called 'hormesis'; in essence the body's cells respond well to stress and become stronger. Individual body cells fix themselves in response to daily wear and tear, but seem to do so more effectively after being in a fasted state, just as muscles after exercise are temporarily damaged, but swiftly repair themselves. Hormesis may therefore reduce the development of cancerous cells and slow down the ageing process, contributing to 5:2's wider health benefits. It seems that this effect might be cumulative too so that the more fast periods that your body experiences, the stronger the cells become.

Slowing the ageing process
Professor Valter Longo at the University of California has shown that fasting reduces blood circulation of a hormone called insulin-like growth factor (IGF-1). IGF-1 may over-stimulate body cells to grow and regenerate in later life, contributing to early ageing and cancerous growth. Dr Mark Mattson, a neuroscientist at the National Institute of Ageing in Baltimore, is also interested in the potential of fasting diets to protect against Parkinson's, Alzheimer's and degenerative brain disorders, often linked to old age. It is theoretically possible, therefore, that including fasting days from early adulthood onwards will slow the effects of ageing, although devising research to investigate this theory would be problematic.

Protecting against impaired glucose tolerance and diabetes
In both human and animal studies, the hormone insulin seems to perform better after fasting. This might be because reducing fat around the waist seems to help insulin to work more efficiently. This is very helpful in keeping sugar levels controlled, and preventing Impaired Glucose Tolerance, which can lead to irreversible Type 2 diabetes.

Inflammatory diseases
Fasting seems to increase body cells' production of beneficial antioxidants, which is good for keeping them intact, and for their longer term health. Healthier cells are less likely to become damaged and so the body is less prone to inflammatory diseases.

◀ Research has shown that a reduced waist measurement helps insulin work more effectively.

Acid reflux

Excess weight, spicy foods, alcohol and caffeine can contribute to acid reflux, producing a burning sensation at the top of the stomach after mealtimes. It is often treated with medication, but lower food intakes will naturally decrease the amount of stomach acid produced, so may help prevent or reduce acid reflux on fasting days.

Blood cholesterol

Cholesterol levels are affected by many things, including liver production, weight and diet. Intermittent fasting seems to help lower both total blood cholesterol and 'bad' Low Density Lipoprotein (LDL) levels, which helps decrease the risk of heart disease and strokes.

A natural high

Physiological factors, including endorphins and brain-derived neurotropic factor (BNDF), may contribute to feelings of alertness, well-being, contentment and a natural 'high' when food is

▲ Smaller portions of freshly cooked meals that are nutritionally balanced can offer wider health benefits than just weight loss.

restricted. A positive feeling of empowerment may also come from knowing that you are no longer being controlled by food.

Sensory food enjoyment

It is probably not surprising that intermittent dieting converts report a heightened sense of taste and simple sensory enjoyment of food. Savouring every mouthful we eat, in order to improve our mental and physical satisfaction, can help prevent overeating.

Increased knowledge

Intermittent dieting is great for learning about the fundamentals of balancing food intake and gaining an understanding about energy and hunger to get you through fasting days. People with this insight into food have more success keeping the weight off than those who don't.

TIME TO START FASTING

Now that you're aware of the science behind intermittent fasting, and the possible benefits, it's time to take the plunge and start to introduce it into your week.

Intermittent fasting – one diet fits all?

This type of weight loss programme is great for healthy adults with the self-discipline to plan their meals and drinks adequately on fasting days, but it is not suitable for everyone and you should consider potential limitations before you start.

Since your sleep and ability to concentrate may be affected, fasting diets are not advisable where concentration is critical to the safety of others, particularly during the early days of the diet when your body may be less well adapted.

▼ It is easy to adapt low-calorie recipes to feed other members of the family, by adding extra protein or an accompaniment of carbohydrates.

That said there are many people who do responsible, skilled work in the military, teaching and health professions who cope perfectly well, and report feelings of empowerment and elation while fasting. Strenuous exercise when fasting may also leave you feeling weak, particularly if you are not used to it.

Common sense, and medical opinion, suggest that the diet is also not suitable for teenagers, diabetics, those with kidney issues, pregnant women, or anyone with a history of eating disorders. If in doubt, it is always advisable to discuss any significant changes to your diet or exercise regimen ideally with your doctor, or a registered health professional.

If you are a parent, it is good to encourage children to have an interest in healthy eating. They shouldn't be involved in calorie counting and fasting, however, which is certainly not recommended for growing children.

▲ Flavour your fast day foods with fresh-tasting herbs and pungent spices.

Getting started

First, use an online calculator to work out what your Body Mass Index (BMI) is, and what it should be. Once you have this, work out how much you need to lose. It would be realistic to expect to lose around 0.5kg/1lb weekly on a 5:2 regimen. A 1.66m/5'5" woman weighing 80kg/12 stone 7lbs (BMI = 29.1) would need to reach a target weight of 63.25kg/9 stone 9lbs, to achieve a BMI of 23, which is a loss of 16.75kg/2 stone 9 lbs. If losing 0.5kg/1lb a week this would take 37 weeks.

Overcoming challenges

The advice in this book for starting out, sticking to and succeeding with intermittent fasting, will guide you through the challenging early days, but also later on when focus may be waning. There may be some testing times. As with anything, keeping focused, whether it be a wedding, a beach holiday, improved health, or simply feeling more positive about yourself, is hugely important. Consider getting the support of a 5:2 buddy to talk to if the going gets tough.

FIRST DAY TIPS

• Pick your first fasting day when you are busy; the best way to forget about hunger pangs is to have something to do. Don't choose a high-pressure day, however, when you need patience and concentration.
• Use online resources or smartphone apps to help you record your calorie intake and activity.
• Invest in some digital kitchen scales that weigh in small quantities, to make sure that you're accurate in the kitchen.
• Plan your fasting day before you begin.
• Don't go food shopping on a fasting day; supermarkets are designed to tempt you to buy, with piped food smells, offers, and point of sale displays.
• When you start to feel hungry, drink a glass of water, phone a friend, or simply wait for just 15 minutes, as often the hunger goes away.
• A small amount of the right kind of fat, and plenty of flavourings, makes food more appetizing and more satisfying, so plan these into your meals.
• The first fasting day is often the worst; after this your body and emotions will adapt to feeling hungry, as you realise it's not something to be frightened of.

Non-fasting days

There is often an assumption that people who fast one day will inevitably overeat the next, but studies on intermittent dieters indicate that this is usually not the case. This is possibly because awareness of real hunger is quickly learned, or that after just 24 hours the stomach starts to shrink, so perceived 'stomach' hunger is less. Cravings for sugar are also considerably reduced.

HOW TO STRUCTURE YOUR FAST DAY

There are quite a few options for planning eating on fasting days, depending on daily commitments and personal preference. No specific programme is better than another, and some are slightly longer because of night times, but what is important is that you can manage to stick to your calorie restriction, and still follow a normal routine. On a day when you're not working and are going to have a long lie in, for example, you can plan to have a really late breakfast, or brunch, then not eat again until the evening.

Morning start

It is a good idea to fast on days when you have a standard routine and are busy without being unusually stressed or overworked. If you are going to work, for example, you will probably start fasting first thing in the morning, in which case you might have a light breakfast and lunch, and a more substantial dinner. You might find it quite easy to eat very little during the day, however, and decide to graze on a few crudités, saving your calories for a larger supper.

Midday start

If you begin fasting in the middle of the day you should eat your usual breakfast then a calorie-controlled lunch and dinner, and the next morning, a calorie-controlled breakfast. You are then back to normal eating by lunch on the second day.

Evening start

This is a convenient way to work around occasions where it is difficult to fast. Eat your usual evening meal at 6pm, and a fasting breakfast and lunch the next day. You are able to eat normally by 8pm the following day.

Eating on the move

There will be times when you are fasting when you are out, and need to find a calorie-controlled snack. You should find it easier, with practice, to plan suitable meals and snacks at home and take your food with you. The lists on the opposite page give some ideas that you can easily transport, or purchase when out.

Recipe flexibility

The recipes in this book usually serve two or four people. Some dishes are difficult to make for just one person, but can be shared with non-fasting people. However many of the recipes will keep very well, either refrigerated or frozen, and bulk cooking is a good idea for getting ahead on fasting days. Some dishes are suitable for a family supper, and we give suggestions for accompaniments for any non-fasting diners.

Scaling down recipes is equally easy, as the nutritional analysis is given per portion. Simply halve or quarter the ingredients for one person to get the same calorie count. If you want to substitute ingredients, do so, but make use of the food charts to make sure that calorie counts match: for example, in a stir-fry, swap 85g/3oz chicken for 115g/4oz of prawns (shrimp), or substitute 55g/2oz basmati rice for the same weight of couscous.

Finally, don't try to keep a completely balanced diet on fasting days as this will not be possible on such a low-calorie intake. You should, however, structure your daily intake to include at least one portion of protein, a very small amount of carbohydrate and as many portions of vegetables or salad as you can. There should also be a little oil or fat. You should, of course, also consume plenty of calorie-free fluids throughout the day.

30-CALORIE SNACKS

200g/7oz cucumber sticks

150g/5½ oz cherry tomatoes

400g/14oz celery sticks

1 8g/⅓oz rice cake

6g/¼oz 70 per cent dark (bittersweet) chocolate

1 whole brazil nut (4g/⅙oz)

8oz/200g drained gherkins

1 clementine (75g/3oz when peeled)

55g/2oz grapes

110g/4oz strawberries

1 small kiwi fruit (55g/2oz peeled)

55g/2oz carrot batons with 5ml/1 tsp hummus

55g/2oz blueberries

coffee with 60mls/4 tbsp semi-skimmed (low-fat) milk

2 marshmallows (10g/⅓oz)

5g/⅕oz unsweetened popcorn

7.5ml/½ tbsp dry roasted pumpkin seeds

50-CALORIE SNACKS

100g/3½oz apple

100g/3½oz cherries

50g/2oz pitted green olives

1 30g/1oz wholegrain crispbread with 5ml/1 tsp low-fat cream cheese

miso soup made with a 15g/½oz instant miso sachet and just-boiled water

1 large pitted date (15g/½oz)

20g/⅔oz raisins

5 'stack' crisps (US potato chips) (10g/⅓oz total weight)

8g/⅓oz peanuts

1 slice wholemeal (whole-wheat) bread (28g/1oz)

1 pot natural (plain) yogurt (115g/4oz)

1 small boiled egg

3 walnut halves (10g/½oz)

150ml/5fl oz glass of skimmed milk or rice milk

20g/⅔oz low-fat cheddar

1 jaffa cake (12g/½oz)

100-CALORIE SNACKS

100g/3½oz banana

4 dried figs (85g/3oz)

3 chocolate finger biscuits (cookies) (15g/½oz)

banana shake made with 55g/2oz banana and 100ml/3½fl oz semi-skimmed (low-fat) milk

110g/4oz strawberries with 30g/1oz half-fat crème fraiche

1 slice wholemeal (whole-wheat) bread (28g/1oz) with 55g/2oz baked beans

45g/1½oz sliced ham

1 17g/¾oz oatcake with 2.5ml/½ tsp peanut butter

2 20g/¾oz chocolate-covered rice cakes

25g/1oz unsweetened cereal with 40ml/1½fl oz skimmed milk

14g/½oz whole cashew nuts

1 17g/¾oz chocolate digestive or 2 oreo cookies

½ can (200g/7oz) tomato soup

40g/1½oz feta cheese

LONG TERM SUCCESS

It is not recommended that two fasting days are done consecutively; it will be very challenging, without any scientifically proven advantage. Your chosen fasting days can, however, change to fit the demands on your time, week to week, although many people like to stick to the same ones.

After a couple of fasting days you'll learn to tell the difference between 'head' and 'tummy' hunger. Head hunger often happens when we see or smell tempting food and drink, even when we've eaten a good meal. Tummy hunger – a grumbling stomach – may be real, but train yourself to be resilient, remembering that tomorrow you won't be fasting.

Fasting periods
You can start your 24-hour fasting period at times to suit you, for example lunchtime to lunchtime, or mid-morning or mid-morning. The advantage of this is that you can fit it around your lifestyle to suit and enjoy social engagements or professional obligations. Don't over-compensate by making up for larger meals outside the fasting period.

▲ Flavouring food with fresh herbs and roasted spices adds to the enjoyment of a meal.

Exercise on fasting days
Light to moderate exercise on fasting days will help weight loss by using energy and diverting you from eating. Exercise, along with plenty of fibre-rich fruit, vegetables and grains, and plenty of fluid each day will also help keep your bowel movements regular.

You will probably need to increase your fluid intake on fasting days, even without exercise, as you won't be getting so much water from food.

Still enjoying food on fast days
Include moderate amounts of salty foods on fasting days, for example smoked fish, cured ham, well-seasoned soups, soy sauce and yeast

◀ Non-strenuous exercise such as yoga is a good idea on fasting days, but make sure you don't overdo it.

extract. While this may be contrary to general health advice on sodium levels, the body loses more sodium when burning fat, so a little more may be necessary to help hydration and prevent headaches. You should not include these if you are on a diuretic tablet for high blood pressure. Be adventurous with your use of herbs and spices, which will bring fresh tastes, variety and pleasure to your food.

Although lower-fat dairy foods can save precious calories, some brands that are marked 'low-fat' have a large quantity of added sugars so check the labels carefully. Use semi-skimmed (low-fat) or skimmed milk in drinks or on muesli, and select low-fat but plain yogurts, or leave dairy out completely on fast days.

Eating a 'rainbow' of lots of different coloured fruits and vegetables on non-fast days helps to ensure the intake of a range of nutrients and antioxidants. You can also minimize nutrient losses to the fruits and vegetables by buying fresh, organic produce, eating vegetables raw, or steaming them to retain vitamins.

REGULAR FASTING TIPS
- Zero-kcalorie noodles, made from the Konjac plant, are increasingly available and are a very useful almost kcalorie-free accompaniment to our recipes
- If you can't bear black tea or coffee, measure out 100ml/3½fl oz/½ cup skimmed milk (45 calories) to use in tea or coffee through the day.
- Avoid alcohol; it can increase hunger, and adds on huge amounts of calories.
- Use convenience foods with care, and check the nutritional values on the packaging. Ready meals and sauces have hidden fats and high levels of salt and sugars.
- Mix raw vegetables with cooked, for texture interest. Just before serving, grate a little garlic into stir-fries, or scatter a few salted roasted seeds on soups or salads for a final flavour burst.

▼ Strong flavours, like smoked fish, will satisfy your appetite more than bland tastes.

▼ Keeping busy on a fasting day will stop you thinking about food and keep your mental hunger at bay.

FOOD CHARTS

This table of calorie values will help you work out your own meals, or adapt the recipes in this book. We have given protein values too, which is important as it helps to satisfy appetite.

MEAT/FISH/TOFU	Portion/quantity	Kcalories	Protein (g)
skinless chicken, poached	85g/3oz	128	32
skinless duck breast, roasted	85g/3oz	195	27
pork loin chop (lean), grilled/broiled	85g/3oz	156	25
bacon (lean), grilled/broiled	55g/2oz	160	13
veal fillet, grilled/broiled	85g/3oz	195	27
liver, braised	85g/3oz	170	21
beef, fillet steak, grilled/broiled	85g/3oz	160	25
beef, roasted	85g/3oz	171	27
ham, cooked	85g/3oz	100	16
cod loin, baked	115g/4oz	110	25
sea bass, baked	115g/4oz	111	21
salmon steak, grilled/broiled	85g/3oz	182	21
haddock, grilled/broiled	115g/4oz	120	30
fresh tuna, grilled/broiled	85g/3oz	115	19
sardines, grilled/broiled	85g/3oz	162	21
anchovies, canned, drained	28g/1oz	48	6
tuna, canned in brine, drained	65g/2½oz	64	15
prawns (shrimp), cooked	55g/2oz	63	12
scallops, steamed	x6 small/55g/2oz	70	14
tofu, uncooked	55g/2oz	63	7

CARBOHYDRATES	Portion/quantity	Kcalories	Protein (g)
bread, white	1 slice/36g/1½oz	78	3
bread, seeded/granary	1 slice/36g/1½oz	85	4
pitta bread, wholegrain	x1/85g/3oz	181	7
pasta, uncooked	55g/2oz/½ cup	188	7
egg noodles, uncooked	55g/2oz/½ cup	215	7
basmati rice, uncooked	55g/2oz/¼ cup	198	4
arborio rice, uncooked	55g/2oz/¼ cup	190	4
couscous, uncooked	55g/2oz/¼ cup	203	7
oats, uncooked	55g/2oz/¼ cup	220	7
pearl barley, uncooked	55g/2oz/⅓ cup	198	4

quinoa, uncooked	55g/2oz/⅓ cup	205	13
spelt, uncooked	55g/2oz/¼ cup	186	3
potato, new, boiled in skin	160g/6oz	105	2
potato, baked	115g/4oz	156	4
sweet potato, baked	115g/4oz	132	2

DAIRY	Portion/quantity	Kcalories	Protein (g)
milk, whole (full-fat)	100ml/3½fl oz/scant ½ cup	65	3
milk, semi-skimmed (low-fat)	100ml/3½fl oz/scant ½ cup	46	3
milk, skimmed	100ml/3½fl oz/scant ½ cup	35	3
milk, coconut, light	60ml/4 tbsp	60	trace
yogurt, natural (plain)	115g/4oz/½ cup	64	6
crème fraîche	15ml/1 tbsp	56	1
crème fraîche, low-fat	15ml/1 tbsp	24	1
cheddar cheese	40g/1½oz	166	10
cheddar cheese, low-fat	40g/1½oz	110	13
Edam cheese	40g/1½oz	133	10
feta cheese	40g/1½oz	100	6
mozzarella	40g/1½oz	115	10
Parmesan, grated	15ml/1 tbsp	22	6
cream cheese	15ml/1 tbsp	131	1
cream cheese, low-fat	15ml/1 tbsp	24	2
cottage cheese	15ml/1 tbsp	30	4
cheese spread	15ml/1 tbsp	80	4
mayonnaise	15ml/1 tbsp	118	trace
mayonnaise, low-fat	15ml/1 tbsp	43	trace

VEGETABLES/SALAD/PULSES	Portion/quantity	Kcalories	Protein (g)
asparagus	x2 spears/55g/2oz	14	2
aubergine (eggplant)	55g/2oz	8	trace
beansprouts	55g/2oz/½ cup	17	2
beetroot (beets)	55g/2oz	20	1
broccoli	55g/2oz	18	2
Brussels sprouts	x6/55g/2oz	23	2
butternut squash	55g/2oz	20	1
carrot	55g/2oz	17	trace
cauliflower	55g/2oz	18	2
cabbage, Savoy	55g/2oz	15	1

cabbage, red	55g/2oz	12	1
celery	x1 stick/55g/2oz	4	trace
chard, Swiss	55g/2oz	10	trace
corn	55g/2oz/2 tbsp	52	2
courgette (zucchini)	55g/2oz	11	1
daikon (white radish)	55g/2oz	9	2
fennel	55g/2oz	6	trace
green beans	55g/2oz	12	1
leek	55g/2oz	7	1
mangetouts (snow peas)	55g/2oz	17	2
mushrooms	55g/2oz	7	1
okra	55g/2oz	17	2
pak choi (bok choy)	55g/2oz	6	1
parsnip	55g/2oz	35	1
peas	55g/2oz/2 tbsp	46	4
pepper (bell)	55g/2oz	15	2
pumpkin	55g/2oz	7	trace
spinach	55g/2oz	14	2
sugar snap peas	55g/2oz	18	2
avocado	½ average pear/85g/3oz	161	1
cucumber	115g/4oz	20	1
lettuce, cos	4 leaves/28g/1oz	4	trace
rocket (arugula)	handful/28g/1oz	8	1
spring onions (scallions)	x3/55g/2oz	13	1
tomato	1 medium/85g/3oz	14	1
watercress	55g/2oz	12	2
chickpeas, canned/drained	55g/2oz/2 tbsp	63	4
kidney beans, canned/drained	55g/2oz/2 tbsp	55	4
Puy lentils, cooked	55g/2oz/2 tbsp	63	5

FRESH FRUIT	Portion/quantity	Kcalories	Protein (g)
apple	115g/4oz	51	trace
apricot, stoned (pitted)	55g/2oz	17	trace
banana	100g/3½oz	95	1
blueberries	55g/2oz	31	trace
cherries, stoned (pitted)	100g/3½oz	48	1
clementine	55g/2oz	25	trace
fig	55g/2oz	23	1
grapefruit half	55g/2oz	18	trace
grapes	55g/2oz	33	trace
kiwi fruit	55g/2oz	27	1
mango	85g/3oz	43	trace
melon, galia	2cm/1in slice/55g/2oz	13	trace
peach, stoned (pitted)	115g/4oz	36	1
pear	150g/5oz	60	1
pineapple	55g/2oz	22	trace
plum, stoned (pitted)	55g/2oz	20	trace
pomegranate seeds	55g/2oz/½ cup	45	1
raspberries	x14/55g/2oz	14	1
strawberries	x5/55g/2oz	15	trace

NUTS/SEEDS/DRIED FRUIT	Portion/quantity	Kcalories	Protein (g)
brazil nuts	x3/12g/⅓oz	81	2
cashew nuts	x10/10g/⅓oz	57	2
almonds	x6/10g/⅓oz	61	2
pistachios	x10/10g/⅓oz	60	2
peanuts	x10/10g/⅓oz	56	3
walnuts	x3 halves/20g/⅔oz	69	1
pumpkin seeds	15ml/1 tbsp	80	3
sesame seeds	15ml/1 tbsp	60	2
linseed/flaxseeds	15ml/1 tbsp	67	3
sunflower seeds	15ml/1 tbsp	87	3
apricot, dried	28g/1oz	47	1
cranberries, dried	28g/1oz	44	trace
date, dried	28g/1oz	41	trace
fig, dried	28g/1oz	57	1
raisins	28g/1oz/1 tbsp	68	1
pineapple	28g/1oz	69	1

FAST DAY EATING PLANS

The following plans offer structured days of balanced dishes that keep within 500 calories. Various start and finish times allow the flexibility to start at different times of the day to enable you to fit in other commitments. Some days include a 35-calorie allowance of skimmed milk for hot drinks, whereas others assume that you will drink calorie-free fluids, and there are ideas for men to increase the plans by 100 calories.

Given the flexible start times, it is realistic that you might include a larger meal or snack prior to the start of the fast period. While this is accepted as a way of managing hunger, do be mindful that high-calorie meals at any time will slow your rate of weight loss. It is also possible that fast periods may be more than 24 hours if sleeping comes at the beginning or end of a fast day. Since sleep may be disrupted by fasting, you may want to include a snack or light meal at the end of a fast day before bedtime. This should be low in sugar and include some protein; see our food charts or snack lists for ideas.

MIDDAY START PLANS

501 Kcal	**495** Kcal
LUNCH	**LUNCH**
Fragrant Mushrooms on Lettuce, p146, 75kcal	Hot drink with half milk allowance
MID-AFTERNOON	**MID-AFTERNOON**
	Any 30-calorie snack
DINNER	**DINNER**
Chinese Duck Stir-Fry, p127, 263kcal	Spicy Tortilla, p116, 266kcal
SUPPER	**SUPPER**
Raspberry Granita, p65, 80kcal	Hot drink, no milk
BREAKFAST	**BREAKFAST**
Instant Popped Amaranth Cereal, p35, 83kcal	Crunchy Oat Cereal, p35, 164kcal
MID-MORNING	**MID-MORNING**
	Hot drink with half milk allowance
SKIMMED MILK ALLOWANCE	**SKIMMED MILK ALLOWANCE**
0	100ml/3½fl oz/⅓ cup, 35kcals
100-CALORIE SUPPLEMENT FOR MEN	**100-CALORIE SUPPLEMENT FOR MEN**
Add half a regular-sized pitta bread, 32g = 95kcal, to Fragrant Mushrooms	Slice a medium banana, 100kcal, onto the Crunchy Oat Cereal

MIDDAY START PLANS

496 Kcal	**502** Kcal
LUNCH	**LUNCH**
Chilli Salad Omelette Wrap, p117, 168kcal	Quinoa Salmon Frittata, p113, 215kcal
MID-AFTERNOON	**MID-AFTERNOON**
Hot drink, no milk	
DINNER	**DINNER**
Warm Bean Salad, p144, 219kcal	
SUPPER	**SUPPER**
Hot drink, no milk	Cashew Chicken Stir-Fry, p126, 287kcal
BREAKFAST	**BREAKFAST**
Quinoa Granola Bar, p36, 109kcal	
MID-MORNING	**MID-MORNING**
Hot drink, no milk	
SKIMMED MILK ALLOWANCE	**SKIMMED MILK ALLOWANCE**
0	0
100-CALORIE SUPPLEMENT FOR MEN	**100-CALORIE SUPPLEMENT FOR MEN**
Cook 30g/1oz pasta to serve with Warm Bean Salad	85g/3oz sweet potato, baked, with 2.5ml/½ tsp low-fat cream cheese with Chicken Stir-Fry

EVENING START PLANS

500 Kcal	**508** Kcal
DINNER	**DINNER**
Stir-Fried Squid with Vegetables, p124, 165kcal	Spelt with Vegetables and Pancetta, p157, 253kcal
SUPPER	**SUPPER**
Poached Pear, p63, 89kcal and a hot drink, no milk	
BREAKFAST	**BREAKFAST**
Hot drink, with half milk allowance	Muesli, p34, 153kcal
MID-MORNING	**MID-MORNING**
Apple and Leaf Lift Off, p56, 68kcal	
LUNCH	**LUNCH**
Hot drink, with half milk allowance	Pak Choi with Lime Dressing, p152, 102kcal
MID-AFTERNOON	**MID-AFTERNOON**
Tabbouleh, p54, 143kcal	
SKIMMED MILK ALLOWANCE	**SKIMMED MILK ALLOWANCE**
100ml/3½fl oz/⅓ cup, 35kcals	0
100-CALORIE SUPPLEMENT FOR MEN	**100-CALORIE SUPPLEMENT FOR MEN**
Have a small boiled egg with a small slice of bread, no butter, for breakfast	Cook 25g/1oz quinoa and serve with the Pak Choi for lunch

EVENING START PLANS

502 Kcal	**490** Kcal
DINNER	**DINNER**
Stir-Fried Prawns, p125, 161kcal	Clear Soup with Seafood Sticks, p72, 34kcal
SUPPER	**SUPPER**
	Hot drink, no milk
BREAKFAST	**BREAKFAST**
Baked Ham and Eggs, p120, 216kcal	1 Herby Seeded Oatcakes, p38, 62kcal and Carrot and Citrus Juice, p60, 85kcal
MID-MORNING	**MID-MORNING**
	Hot drink, no milk
LUNCH	**LUNCH**
Velvety Pumpkin Soup, p76, 125kcal	Chicken Pitta, p49, 209kcal
MID-AFTERNOON	**MID-AFTERNOON**
	Any 100-calorie snack
SKIMMED MILK ALLOWANCE	**SKIMMED MILK ALLOWANCE**
0	0
100-CALORIE SUPPLEMENT FOR MEN	**100-CALORIE SUPPLEMENT FOR MEN**
Add a medium-sized seeded roll with the soup for lunch	Add another ½ portion of Chicken Pitta to lunch

MORNING START PLANS

492 Kcal	506 Kcal
BREAKFAST	**BREAKFAST**
Porridge, p34, 160kcal, with third of milk allowance	Hot drink, no milk
MID-MORNING	**MID-MORNING**
Hot drink with third of milk allowance	Smoked Salmon and Chive Omelette, p43, 180kcal
LUNCH	**LUNCH**
Haricot Bean Soup, p78, 213kcal	
MID-AFTERNOON	**MID-AFTERNOON**
	Any 50-calorie snack
DINNER	**DINNER**
Beetroot Orange Salad, p144, 84kcal	Thai Beef Stew, p108, 187kcal
SUPPER	**SUPPER**
Hot drink with third of milk allowance	2 x Almond and Cardamom Macaroons, p62, 92kcal
SKIMMED MILK ALLOWANCE	**SKIMMED MILK ALLOWANCE**
100ml/3½fl oz/⅓ cup, 35kcals	0
100-CALORIE SUPPLEMENT FOR MEN	**100-CALORIE SUPPLEMENT FOR MEN**
Small roll with a scrape of low-fat spread 98kcal	Cook 25g/1oz/2 tbsp basmati rice and serve with Thai Beef Stew

MORNING START PLANS

491 Kcal

BREAKFAST

Banana,
100kcal

MID-MORNING

Hot drink, no milk

LUNCH

Marinated Sashimi Style
Tuna, p86, 111kcal

MID-AFTERNOON

DINNER

Baked Peppers with Puy
Lentils, p156, 130kcal, with
Courgette and Potato Bake,
p158, 150kcal

SUPPER

Hot drink, no milk

SKIMMED MILK ALLOWANCE

0

100-CALORIE SUPPLEMENT FOR MEN

Add 115g/4oz natural
yogurt with grated,
medium apple to breakfast

492 Kcal

BREAKFAST

Mango and Lime Lassi,
p40, 85kcal

MID-MORNING

Hot drink with half milk
allowance

LUNCH

Frittata with Sun Dried
Tomatoes, p114, 231kcal

MID-AFTERNOON

Hot drink, with half milk
allowance

DINNER

SUPPER

Butter Bean Soup,
p79, 141kcal

SKIMMED MILK ALLOWANCE

100ml/3½fl oz/⅓ cup,
35kcals

100-CALORIE SUPPLEMENT FOR MEN

Half a toasted muffin with a
scrape of low-fat cream
cheese at supper

BREAKFASTS

A sensible breakfast or brunch can be critical on fasting days, and this chapter gives you plenty of inspiration for starting your fasting period. Most of the recipes serve two, as portion control is of course critical on fasting days, but you can enjoy these healthy dishes on non-fasting days with larger portions. Prepare cereals in bulk, as suggested, as they will keep well in good-quality airtight containers. If you're not hungry when you get up, wait before you eat, and take a breakfast bar or freshly-made smoothie with you.

◀ Crunchy oat cereal.
▼ Papaya, lime and ginger salad.

PORRIDGE

160 Calories

A very versatile start to the day, porridge can be made with water and served on its own, or made with milk and served with honey and cream. For a fast day, a helping of water-based porridge will keep you going until lunchtime, but only uses up around 160 calories. Add salt, and a sprinkling of cinnamon for flavour.

40g/1½oz rolled oats
good pinch of salt
cinnamon, for serving

Serves 1

NUTRITIONAL INFORMATION: Energy 160kcal/668.8kJ; Protein 5g; Carbohydrate 26g, of which sugars 0g; Fat 3g, of which saturates 0g; Cholesterol 0mg; Calcium 21mg; Fibre 3g; Sodium 743mg

1 Weigh the correct amount of oats and then transfer to a cup. Pour the oats into a pan, and use the cup to add two and a half times the amount of water to oats. Add salt to taste.

2 Place the pan on a medium heat and bring to the boil, stirring. Reduce the heat, and simmer for 3–4 minutes until thickened. Pour into a bowl, and sprinkle with a little cinnamon.

Variation Add a 25g/1oz blueberries (15kcal) if you wish, but remember to add them to your calorie count.

MUESLI

153 Calories

Make a large batch of this muesli, as it keeps well, and have a small portion for a sustaining fast day breakfast. Moisten with a splash of diluted orange juice or milk.

270g/10oz/3 cups rolled oats
115g/4oz/1 cup of macadamia nuts,
    flaked almonds and cashews
150g/5oz/1 cup sunflower seeds
75g/3oz/½ cup raisins
75g/3oz/½ cup dried cranberries

Makes 20 fast-day servings

NUTRITIONAL INFORMATION: Energy 153kcal/639.54kJ; Protein 4g; Carbohydrate 18g, of which sugars 6g; Fat 8g, of which saturates 1g; Cholesterol 0mg; Calcium 19mg; Fibre 2g; Sodium 8mg

1 Place the nuts in a bowl or a sealed plastic bag and break into large pieces with the end of a rolling pin.

2 Transfer the nuts to a dry frying pan, and toast on a low heat until lightly golden. Leave to cool completely.

3 Tip the oats, seeds, raisins and cranberries into an airtight container. Add the cooled nuts and mix. Serve with a little fruit juice or yogurt. The muesli will keep for up to two weeks.

Fasting tip Just 30ml/2 tbsp of this muesli is the correct portion size for a fasting day.

CRUNCHY OAT CEREAL

164 Calories

This is a good store-cupboard standby for ordinary days, and for fast days when you want to have a slow-release breakfast. When fasting, you should measure your serving size carefully, and eat it moistened with a little weak black tea, or with 60ml/4 tbsp of skimmed milk, which would add 26 calories.

200g/7oz/1¾ cups rolled oats
150g/5oz/1¼ cups mixed nuts,
    roughly chopped
30ml/2 tbsp maple syrup
30ml/2 tbsp vegetable oil

Makes 24 fast-day servings

NUTRITIONAL INFORMATION: Energy 164kcal/685.52kJ; Protein 4g; Carbohydrate 14g, of which sugars 2g; Fat 11g, of which saturates 1g; Cholesterol 0mg; Calcium 32mg; Fibre 2g; Sodium 7mg

1 Preheat oven to 160°C/325°F/Gas 3. Mix all the ingredients together and spread on to a large baking tray.

2 Bake for 30–35 minutes, or until golden and crunchy. Leave to cool, then break up into clumps and serve. Store in an airtight container.

Fasting tip Around 32ml/2 tbsp of this cereal is the correct sized portion for a fasting day.

INSTANT POPPED AMARANTH CEREAL

83 Calories

High in protein, B-vitamins and minerals, amaranth is a nutrient-packed way to start the day as a delicious topping for yogurt; 45ml/3 tbsp plain yogurt is 25 calories.

20g/¾oz amaranth grain
2.5ml/½ tsp clear honey
2.5ml/½ tsp ground cinnamon
natural (plain) yogurt, to serve

Serves 1

NUTRITIONAL INFORMATION: Energy 83kcal/346.94kJ; Protein 3g; Carbohydrate 15g, of which sugars 3g; Fat 1g, of which saturates Trace; Cholesterol 0mg; Calcium 69mg; Fibre 1g; Sodium 2mg

1 Heat a heavy pan over a medium heat, with the lid on. Place half the amaranth grain in the pan and shake to form a thin layer of grains. The popping should start immediately.

2 Gently shake the pan to ensure even distribution of heat so that the grains do not burn. When the popping stops, remove the pan from the heat and pour the amaranth into a bowl.

3 Repeat with the other half of the grain and add to the bowl. Add the cinnamon and honey and mix. Serve as it is, or use as a topping for yogurt.

QUINOA GRANOLA BARS

109 Calories

If you leave the house without breakfast, take one of these with you so that when you do need to eat you have a nutritious snack to hand. Quinoa is a nutrient-rich supergrain, which is now also sold in a puffed form.

150ml/¼ pint/⅔ cup clear honey
25g/1oz butter
2 small or 1 large eating apple,
    peeled and grated
30ml/2 tbsp puffed quinoa
30ml/2 tbsp ground flaxseeds
    (linseeds)
30ml/2 tbsp roughly chopped
    hazelnuts
2.5ml/½ tsp ground cloves
5ml/1 tsp mixed (apple pie) spice
10ml/2 tsp ground ginger

Makes 10

NUTRITIONAL INFORMATION: Energy 109kcal/455.62kJ; Protein 1g; Carbohydrate 15g, of which sugars 13g; Fat 5g, of which saturates 2g; Cholesterol 5mg; Calcium 12mg; Fibre 1g; Sodium 19mg

1 Heat the oven to 180°C/350°F/Gas 4. Grease a 18cm/7in square baking tin (pan), and line with baking parchment.

2 In a large pan over low heat, heat the honey and butter, stirring, until the butter has melted, and you have a thin syrup. Remove the pan from the heat and stir in the remaining ingredients, until thoroughly combined. Transfer to the prepared tin and spread evenly into the edges with the back of a fork.

3 Bake for 30–35 minutes until crisp at the edges. Score into ten bars with a sharp knife while still warm, but leave in the tin until totally cool. Store in an airtight container.

FRUITY BREAKFAST BARS

163 Calories

Store-bought cereal bars are full of sugar, and should be avoided. Try making this quick and easy version, however, which is tastier and more nutritious. The bars can be stored in an airtight container for up to four days or individually frozen.

270g/10oz jar unsweetened apple sauce
115g/4oz/½ cup ready-to-eat dried apricots, chopped
115g/4oz/¾ cup raisins
50g/2oz/¼ cup demerara (raw) sugar
50g/2oz/⅓ cup sunflower seeds
25g/1oz/2 tbsp sesame seeds
25g/1oz/2 tbsp pumpkin seeds
75g/3oz/scant 1 cup rolled oats
75g/3oz/⅔ cup self-rising wholemeal (whole-wheat) flour
50g/2oz/⅔ cup desiccated (dry unsweetened shredded) coconut
2 eggs

Makes 15

NUTRITIONAL INFORMATION: Energy 163kcal/681.34kJ; Protein 5g; Carbohydrate 22g, of which sugars 15g; Fat 7g, of which saturates 3g; Cholesterol 34mg; Calcium 37mg; Fibre 3g; Sodium 25mg

1 Preheat the oven to 200°C/400°F/Gas 6. Lightly grease a 20cm/8in square shallow baking tin (pan) with vegetable oil, and line with baking parchment.

2 Put the apple sauce in a large bowl with the apricots, raisins, sugar and the sunflower, sesame and pumpkin seeds and stir together with a wooden spoon until thoroughly mixed.

3 Add the oats, flour, coconut and eggs to the fruit mixture and gently stir together until combined. Turn the mixture into the tin and spread to the edges in an even layer.

4 Bake for about 25 minutes or until golden and just firm to the touch. Leave to cool in the tin, then lift out on to a board and cut into 15 bars.

HERBY SEEDED OATCAKES

62 Calories

These oatcakes are a great way to stave off hunger pangs, on their own, or with a scrape of low-fat cream cheese. Store in an airtight container.

175g/6oz/1½ cups plain wholemeal (whole-wheat) flour
175g/6oz/1½ cups fine oatmeal
5ml/1 tsp salt
1.5ml/¼ tsp bicarbonate of soda (baking soda)
75g/3oz/6 tbsp white vegetable fat
15ml/1 tbsp fresh thyme leaves, chopped
30ml/2 tbsp sunflower seeds

Makes 32

Fasting tip Make sure you make these oatcakes equal sizes for the correct calorie counts. 5ml/1 tsp low-fat cream cheese adds 8 calories.

NUTRITIONAL INFORMATION: Energy 62kcal/259.16kJ; Protein 2g; Carbohydrate 8g, of which sugars 0g; Fat 3g, of which saturates 1g; Cholesterol 0mg; Calcium 10mg; Fibre 1g; Sodium 99mg

1 Preheat the oven to 150°C/300°F/Gas 2. Line two ungreased baking sheets with baking parchment and set aside.

2 Put the flour, oatmeal, salt and soda in a bowl and rub in the fat until the mixture resembles fine breadcrumbs. Stir in the thyme. Add just enough cold water (about 90–105ml/6–7 tbsp) to the dry ingredients to mix to a stiff but not sticky dough.

3 Gently knead the dough on a lightly floured surface until smooth, then cut roughly in half and roll out one piece on a lightly floured surface to make a 23–25cm/9–10in round.

4 Sprinkle sunflower seeds over the dough and press them in with the rolling pin. Cut into 16 triangles and arrange on one of the baking sheets. Repeat with the remaining dough. Bake for 45–60 minutes until crisp but not brown. Cool on wire racks.

LATE BREAKFAST SMOOTHIE

93 Calories

Tofu is a perfect source of protein, will keep you full for longer, and is also rich in minerals and nutrients. This creamy smoothie should see you through until evening.

115g/4oz firm tofu
115g/4oz strawberries
15ml/1 tbsp sunflower seeds
10ml/2 tsp clear honey
juice of 1 large orange
lemon juice, to serve

Serves 3

NUTRITIONAL INFORMATION: Energy 93kcal/388.74kJ; Protein 6g; Carbohydrate 7g, of which sugars 6g; Fat 4g, of which saturates 1g; Cholesterol 0mg; Calcium 148mg; Fibre 1g; Sodium 3mg

1 Roughly chop the tofu, then hull and roughly chop the strawberries. Reserve a few strawberry chunks.

2 Put the tofu, strawberries, most of the sunflower seeds, honey and orange juice in a blender, and blend until completely smooth, scraping the mixture down from the side of the bowl, if necessary. Pour into tumblers, sprinkle with the sunflower seeds and strawberry chunks, and add a squeeze of lemon.

Fasting tip Breakfast is often eaten out of habit. If you're not hungry when you get up, take this very portable smoothie with you when you leave the house, and drink it when you need to.

RASPBERRY AND OATMEAL SMOOTHIE

68 Calories

Oatmeal gives substance to this tangy, invigorating drink. If you can, prepare it ahead of time as soaking the raw oats helps to break down the starch.

15ml/1 tbsp medium oatmeal
150g/5oz/scant 1 cup raspberries
5ml/1 tsp clear honey
45ml/3 tbsp natural (plain) yogurt

Serves 2

NUTRITIONAL INFORMATION: Energy 68kcal/284.24kJ; Protein 3g; Carbohydrate 12g, of which sugars 7g; Fat 1g, of which saturates 0g; Cholesterol 1mg; Calcium 65mg; Fibre 5g; Sodium 24mg

1 Spoon the oatmeal into a heatproof bowl. Pour in 120ml/ 4fl oz/½ cup boiling water and leave to stand for 10 minutes.

2 Put the soaked oats in a food processor or blender and add the raspberries, honey and about 30ml/2 tbsp of the yogurt. Whizz until smooth and creamy.

3 Pour the raspberry and oatmeal smoothie into a large glass, swirl in the remaining yogurt and top with a few extra raspberries if you wish.

MANGO AND LIME LASSI

This tangy, fruity blend is great for breakfast, with soft, ripe mango blended with yogurt and sharp, zesty lime and lemon juice that is packed with energy.

1 small ripe mango, 250g/9oz total
   weight after peeling
finely grated rind and juice of
   1 lime
5ml/1 tsp lemon juice
50ml/2fl oz/scant ¼ cup natural
   (plain) yogurt
mineral water
lime wedges, to serve

Serves 2

NUTRITIONAL INFORMATION: Energy 85kcal/355.3kJ; Protein 2g; Carbohydrate 20g, of which sugars 19g; Fat Trace, of which saturates 0g; Cholesterol 1mg; Calcium 63mg; Fibre 3g; Sodium 23mg

1 Peel the mango and cut the flesh from the stone (pit). Put the flesh into a blender and add the lime rind and juice.

2 Add the lemon juice, sugar and natural yogurt. Whizz until completely smooth, scraping down the sides once or twice. Stir enough mineral water into the mixture to thin it down and create a drinkable consistency.

3 Serve immediately, with half a lime on the side of each glass so that more juice can be squeezed in if desired.

MUESLI SMOOTHIE   127 Calories

Another great breakfast booster, this store-cupboard smoothie can be an emergency morning breakfast if you've run out of fresh fruit.

1 piece preserved stem ginger
50g/2oz/¼ cup ready-to-eat dried
   apricots, quartered
25g/1oz/¼ cup sugar-free muesli
200ml/7fl oz/1 cup skimmed milk

Serves 2

NUTRITIONAL INFORMATION: Energy 127kcal/530.86kJ; Protein 6g; Carbohydrate 24g; of which sugars 17g; Fat 1g, of which saturates 0g; Cholesterol 3mg; Calcium 151mg; Fibre 5g; Sodium 64mg

1 Chop the ginger and put it in a food processor or blender with the apricots, muesli and milk.

2 Process until smooth, adding more milk if necessary. Serve in tall glasses.

Fasting tip Use a nut-based, sugar-free muesli, such as the one on page 34 for this recipe, so that you get maximum protein and no empty calories from the sugar.

BIG BREAKFAST SMOOTHIE   137 Calories

The body's absorption of natural fruit sugars from this smoothie is slowed down by the fibre-rich wheat bran and sesame seeds.

75g/3oz peeled banana
175g/6oz peeled, diced mango
1 small orange
15ml/1 tbsp wheat bran
5ml/1 tsp sesame seeds

Serves 2

NUTRITIONAL INFORMATION: Energy 137kcal/572.66kJ; Protein 3g; Carbohydrate 30g; of which sugars 25g; Fat 2g, of which saturates Trace; Cholesterol 0mg; Calcium 65mg; Fibre 6g; Sodium 8mg

1 Place the banana and mango in a food processor or blender. Squeeze the juice from the orange and add to the fruit in the food processor or blender.

2 Add the bran, sesame seeds and honey, and whizz until the mixture is smooth and creamy. Pour into glasses and serve.

Fasting tip This isn't such a good portable smoothie as the banana will discolour if you don't drink it soon after mixing.

PAPAYA, LIME AND GINGER SALAD

49 Calories

This refreshing, fruity salad makes a lovely light breakfast, perfect for the summer months. Choose really ripe, fragrant papayas for the best flavour.

1 ripe 350g/12oz papaya
juice of 1 fresh lime
1 piece preserved stem ginger,
   finely sliced

Serves 2

Fasting tip Fruit can be high in calories but peeled papaya is just 31 kcals per 115g/4oz.

NUTRITIONAL INFORMATION: Energy 49kcal/204.82kJ; Protein 2g; Carbohydrate 10g, of which sugars 0g; Fat 0g, of which saturates 0g; Cholesterol 0mg; Calcium 57mg; Fibre 3g; Sodium 26mg

1 Cut the papaya in half lengthways and scoop out the seeds, using a teaspoon. Using a sharp knife, cut the flesh into thin slices and arrange on a platter.

2 Squeeze the lime juice over the papaya and sprinkle with the sliced stem ginger. Serve immediately.

SMOKED SALMON AND CHIVE OMELETTE   180 Calories

The addition of a portion of chopped smoked salmon gives a really luxurious finish to this simple, classic omelette, which makes a great weekend brunch for two.

3 eggs
15ml/1 tbsp low-fat crème fraîche
15ml/1 tbsp chopped fresh chives
50g/2oz smoked salmon, roughly
    chopped
salt and ground black pepper

Serves 2

NUTRITIONAL INFORMATION: Energy 180kcal/752.4kJ; Protein 17g; Carbohydrate Trace, of which sugars 0g; Fat 12g, of which saturates 4g; Cholesterol 350mg; Calcium 62mg; Fibre 0g; Sodium 959mg

1 Beat the eggs until just combined, then stir in the crème fraîche and the chives. Season well with salt and pepper.

2 Heat a medium-sized, non-stick frying pan. Pour in the eggs and cook over a medium heat for 3–4 minutes, drawing the cooked egg from around the edge into the centre of the pan from time to time.

3 At this stage, you can either leave the top of the omelette slightly soft, or finish it off under the grill (broiler), depending on how you like your omelette. Top with the smoked salmon, fold over and cut in half to serve.

SMOKED HADDOCK, SPINACH AND EGG

159 Calories

This makes a good brunch for a late weekend breakfast. The protein in the fish and the egg will keep you going well into the evening, and the spinach gives a superbly, hefty burst of iron and vitamins.

2 x 115g/4oz smoked haddock fillets
115g/4oz fresh spinach, tough
   stalks removed
white wine vinegar
2 eggs
salt and ground black pepper

Serves 2

NUTRITIONAL INFORMATION: Energy 159kcal/664.62kJ; Protein 20g;
Carbohydrate 1g, of which sugars 1g; Fat 8g, of which saturates 2g;
Cholesterol 266mg; Calcium 141mg; Fibre 1g; Sodium 578mg

1 Over a low heat, poach the haddock fillets in a little water, shaking the pan gently to keep the fish moist, for about 5 minutes. When cooked remove the fish and keep warm.

2 Add the spinach to the fish stock in the pan, and wilt for a few minutes, stirring. Season lightly then set aside.

3 To poach the eggs, bring a small pan of water to a simmer and add a few drops of vinegar. Gently crack 1 egg into the water and cook for 3 minutes. Remove using a slotted spoon and place on kitchen paper. Repeat with the second egg. Serve the fish and spinach, topped with an egg.

JUGGED KIPPERS

195 Calories

Kippers – and other smoked fish – are high in taste and protein, and rich in essential omega 3 fats. Jugging is the same as poaching, but easier. On non-fast days, eat these kippers with a knob of butter and crusty bread.

2 kippers (smoked herrings),
   preferably naturally smoked,
   whole or filleted
ground black pepper and lemon
   wedges, to serve

Serves 2

NUTRITIONAL INFORMATION: Energy 195kcal/815.1kJ; Protein 15g;
Carbohydrate 0g, of which sugars 0g; Fat 15g, of which saturates 2g;
Cholesterol 54mg; Calcium 45mg; Fibre 0g; Sodium 706mg

1 Select a jug (pitcher) that is tall enough for the kippers to be completely immersed when the water is added. You can use a large bowl if you prefer. If the kipper heads are still on, remove them.

2 Put the fish into the jug, tails up, and cover them with boiling water. Leave for about 5 minutes, until tender. Drain well and serve the kippers on warmed plates with a little black pepper on each one.

SCRAMBLED EGGS WITH PRAWNS

203 Calories

Freshly scrambled eggs for breakfast or brunch will make an even more enjoyable and sustaining meal if a few succulent prawns are added. If you plan to wait until the evening before eating again you could add another egg (90kcals) to the mixture.

3 spring onions (scallions),
    trimmed and divided into white
    roots and green tops
3 eggs
5ml/1 tsp oil
75g/3oz shelled prawns (shrimp)
15ml/1 tbsp chopped fresh parsley
salt and ground black pepper

Serves 2

NUTRITIONAL INFORMATION: Energy 203kcal/799kJ; Protein 19g; Carbohydrate 1g, of which sugars 1g; Fat 13g, of which saturates 3g; Cholesterol 412mg; Calcium 97mg; Fibre 1g; Sodium 200mg

1 Chop the white of the spring onions and reserve. Very finely slice the green tops.

2 Beat the eggs in a bowl, and season well. In a frying pan, sauté the spring onion whites in the oil on a high heat, then add the prawns. Stir-fry until they turn pink. Reduce the heat and pour in the egg mixture. Cook for about 2 minutes, stirring gently with a wooden spoon.

3 Sprinkle with parsley and about 30ml/2 tbsp sliced green tops. Serve immediately.

SNACKS & JUICES

This chapter offers ideas for quick snacks and energizing vegetable and fruit drinks for an essential pick-up without squandering too many calories. Featuring Mediterranean dips, open sandwiches, salads and vibrant juices, there is plenty to quell hunger pangs without lots of preparation. At the end of the chapter there are a few sweet treats for people who crave a sugar hit, but remember that all sugars, even those naturally occurring in fruit or honey, have the same calories as refined white sugar. Reduced-calorie natural sweeteners can be substituted, but check if they are suitable for baking.

◀ Tabbouleh.
▼ Gazpacho juice.

CHICKEN PITTAS

209 Calories

The chicken in these pitta breads can be hot or cold – either poach or bake two chicken breasts specially, or use up the leftovers from a roast chicken. Choose wholemeal pittas for a more filling, substantial meal. Pittas are around 146 calories, mini pittas are 75. The Moroccan spices here add zero-calorie zest and flavour.

1 small cucumber, peeled
  and diced
3 tomatoes, peeled and chopped
2 spring onions (scallions),
  chopped
5ml/1 tsp olive oil
bunch of flat leaf parsley, chopped
bunch of fresh mint, chopped
½ preserved lemon, finely sliced
15ml/2 tbsp tahini
5ml/1 tsp ground cumin
juice of 1 lemon
2 garlic cloves, crushed
4 mini pitta breads
150g/5oz cooked chicken breast,
  cut into strips
salt and ground black pepper

Serves 4

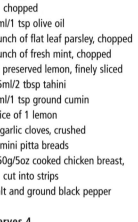

NUTRITIONAL INFORMATION: Energy 209kcal/873.62kJ; Protein 14g; Carbohydrate 22g, of which sugars 4g; Fat 8g, of which saturates 2g; Cholesterol 26mg; Calcium 123mg; Fibre 3g; Sodium 180mg

1 Place the cucumber in a strainer over a bowl, sprinkle with a little salt and leave for 10 minutes to drain. Rinse well and drain again, then place in a bowl with the chopped tomatoes and spring onions.

2 Stir the olive oil, parsley, mint and preserved lemon into the bowl. Season well.

3 In a separate bowl, mix the tahini and cumin with the lemon juice, then thin the mixture down with a little water to the consistency of thick cream. Beat in the garlic and season, adding a little more cumin if you wish.

4 Preheat the grill (broiler) to hot. Lightly toast the pitta breads well away from the heat source until they puff up. (Alternatively, lightly toast the breads in a toaster.) Open the breads and stuff them liberally with the chicken and salad.

Fasting tip For an even lower calorie count, leave out the pitta bread. This is a great salad for assembling in the morning in an airtight container, for a portable office lunch; 1 portion without pitta comes in at 137 calories.

ROASTED PEPPER AND HUMMUS WRAP   158 Calories

Small soft tortillas are just 65 calories, and make a good portable lunch when filled with hummus, made from low GI chickpeas, and tasty roasted pepper.

1 large red (bell) pepper, halved
   and seeded
30ml/2 tbsp hummus
2 x 40g/1½oz tortillas
salt and ground black pepper

Serves 2

NUTRITIONAL INFORMATION: Energy 158kcal/660.44kJ; Protein 5g; Carbohydrate 31g, of which sugars 6g; Fat 3g, of which saturates Trace; Cholesterol 0mg; Calcium 57mg; Fibre 3g; Sodium 216mg

1 Preheat the grill (broiler) to high. Place the pepper halves cut side down on a baking sheet. Grill (broil) for 5 minutes, until charred. Put the pepper halves in a sealed plastic bag and leave to cool.

2 When cooled, remove the peppers from the bag and carefully peel away the charred skin and discard. Thinly slice the flesh using a sharp knife.

3 Spread the hummus over the tortillas in a thin, even layer and top with the roasted pepper slices. Season with salt and plenty of ground black pepper, then roll up and cut in half to serve.

FOCACCIA WITH SARDINES AND TOMATOES   233 Calories

Fresh sardines are a fabulous source of omega 3 fats. They are also filling and satisfying. Canned sardines, drained, could also be used for this recipe.

10 cherry tomatoes
4 fresh sardines
2 x 55g/2oz slices focaccia
salt and ground black pepper

Serves 2

NUTRITIONAL INFORMATION: Energy 233kcal/973.94kJ; Protein 16g; Carbohydrate 22g, of which sugars 3g; Fat 9g, of which saturates 2g; Cholesterol 0mg; Calcium 70mg; Fibre 2g; Sodium 70mg

1 Preheat the oven to 190°C/375°F/Gas 5. Put the cherry tomatoes in a small roasting pan and season with salt and pepper. Roast for 10–15 minutes, or until tender and slightly charred. Remove from the oven and set aside.

2 Preheat the grill (broiler) to high. Place the sardines on a baking sheet and grill (broil) for 4–5 minutes on each side, until cooked through. Remove the fillets from the bones.

3 Split the focaccia in half horizontally and cut each piece in half to give four equal pieces. Toast the cut side under the grill until golden. Top with the sardines and tomatoes and serve.

GRIDDLED TOMATOES ON SODA BREAD

89 Calories

Cooking tomatoes under the grill brings out their taste and sweetness, and releases their juices so that no oil or butter is needed on the toasted soda bread.

2 medium-sized tomatoes, thickly
　sliced
2 x 55g/2oz slices soda bread
balsamic vinegar, for drizzling
salt and ground black pepper

Serves 2

NUTRITIONAL INFORMATION: Energy 89kcal/372.02kJ; Protein 3g; Carbohydrate 19g, of which sugars 6g; Fat 1g, of which saturates Trace; Cholesterol 0mg; Calcium 41mg; Fibre 2g; Sodium 112mg

1 Heat a grill (broiler) to high and line the rack with foil. Grill (broil) the tomato slices for 4–6 minutes, turning once, until softened and slightly charred.

2 Meanwhile, lightly toast the soda bread. Place the tomatoes on top of the toast and drizzle each portion with a little vinegar. Season with salt and ground black pepper and serve.

PICKLED HERRING OPEN SANDWICH

140 Calories

An open sandwich, Danish style, means half the carbohydrates of a standard sandwich. The nutty flavour of dark ryebread is a perfect foil to the herring.

2 x 55g/2oz slices rye bread
2 round (butterhead) lettuce leaves
85g/3oz pickled herring
6 finely sliced salad onion rings
2 parsley sprigs

Serves 2

NUTRITIONAL INFORMATION: Energy 140kcal/585.26kJ; Protein 10g; Carbohydrate 13g, of which sugars 2g; Fat 5g, of which saturates 2g; Cholesterol 21mg; Calcium 52mg; Fibre 2g; Sodium 196mg

1 Top each slice of bread with a lettuce leaf and cut each slice in half.

2 Leaving one curl of lettuce visible on each sandwich, arrange the herring evenly over each of the pieces of bread.

3 Arrange three onion rings over the herring on each sandwich. Garnish by tucking a parsley sprig under the top piece of herring. Serve straight away.

Fasting tip Rye bread, popular in Scandinavia, has a close texture and is rich in soluble fibre, which may help keep cholesterol levels in check.

SMOKED SALMON OPEN SANDWICH

238 Calories

This is another Danish-style sandwich that you can eat on a fasting day. White rye bread has the same health benefits as darker versions.

2 x 55g/2oz slices light rye bread
2 round (butterhead) lettuce leaves
2 x 75g/2oz slices smoked salmon
2 lemon slices
4 dill sprigs

For the mustard sauce
15ml/1 tbsp lemon juice
15ml/1 tbsp Dijon mustard
1 egg yolk
15ml/1 tbsp vegetable oil
5ml/1 tsp chopped fresh dill
salt and ground black pepper

Serves 2

NUTRITIONAL INFORMATION: Energy 238kcal/994.84kJ; Protein 19g; Carbohydrate 13g, of which sugars 2g; Fat 12g, of which saturates 2g; Cholesterol 120mg; Calcium 46mg; Fibre 2g; Sodium 1302mg

1 First make the mustard sauce. In a small bowl, mix together the lemon juice, mustard, egg yolk and oil. Stir in the chopped dill, and season.

2 Top the bread with the lettuce leaves and cut each slice in half. Arrange half a slice of salmon on each half sandwich, folding or rolling the edges to fit.

3 Spoon 5ml/1 tsp mustard sauce down the middle of each sandwich. Cut each lemon slice in half, twist and place in the middle of the salmon. Tuck a dill sprig under each lemon twist, and serve straight away.

SMOKED AUBERGINE DIP

119 Calories

Aubergines, or eggplants, are surprisingly low in calories, unless cooked with oil. This classic Middle Eastern dip has a delicious smoky taste.

250g/9oz aubergine (eggplant)
15ml/1 tbsp tahini
juice of 1 lemon
30ml/2 tbsp natural (plain) yogurt
1 clove garlic, crushed
small bunch of fresh flat leaf
    parsley, finely chopped
sea salt and ground black pepper
10ml/2 tsp olive oil, for drizzling
60g/2oz carrot sticks, optional

Serves 2

NUTRITIONAL INFORMATION: Energy 119kcal/497.42kJ; Protein 3g; Carbohydrate 7g, of which sugars 6g; Fat 9g, of which saturates 2g; Cholesterol 1mg; Calcium 97mg; Fibre 4g; Sodium 26mg

1 Place the aubergines on a hot griddle, or directly over a gas flame, turning from time to time, until they are soft to touch and the skin is charred and flaky. Place them in a plastic bag for a few minutes to sweat and, when cool enough to handle, hold them by the stems under cold running water and peel off the skin. Squeeze out the excess water and chop the flesh to a pulp.

2 Beat the tahini with the lemon juice – the mixture stiffens at first, then loosens to a creamy paste. Beat in the yogurt and then, using a fork, beat in the aubergine pulp.

3 Add the garlic and parsley, season well with salt and pepper and beat the mixture thoroughly. Turn the mixture into a serving dish and drizzle a little olive oil over the top. Eat as it is or with some carrot batons (60g/2oz adds 21 calories).

TABBOULEH

143 Calories

Reducing the bulgur wheat and increasing the parsley makes tabbouleh very low-calorie, and lettuce is virtually calorie-free. For picture, see page 46.

55g/2oz/⅓ cup bulgur wheat
juice of 2 lemons
large bunch of fresh parsley
handful of fresh mint leaves
2–3 tomatoes, finely diced
4 spring onions (scallions), sliced
30ml/2 tbsp olive oil
sea salt and ground black pepper
1 cos or romaine lettuce, trimmed
    and split into leaves, to serve

Serves 4

NUTRITIONAL INFORMATION: Energy 143kcal/597.74 kJ; Protein 3g; Carbohydrate 15g, of which sugars 3g; Fat 8g, of which saturates 1g; Cholesterol 0mg; Calcium 40mg; Fibre 4g; Sodium 9mg

1 Rinse the bulgur in cold water and drain well. Place it in a bowl and pour over the lemon juice. Leave it to soften for 10 minutes while you prepare the salad.

2 Slice the parsley as finely as you can with a sharp knife and place in a bowl. Slice the mint leaves and add them to the bowl with the tomatoes, spring onions and the soaked bulgur. Pour in the oil, season with salt and pepper and toss the salad gently.

OLIVE AND PEPPER SALAD

97 Calories

Tangy and highly-flavoured salads like this are great for keeping in the refrigerator for a quick and easy snack. Serve with a crisped mini pitta (75 calories), if you wish.

2 red or orange (bell) peppers
30ml/2 tbsp black olives
30ml/2 tbsp green olives
1 large tomato, skinned, seeded
  and diced
2 spring onions (scallions),
  trimmed and finely sliced
30ml/2 tbsp olive oil
juice of 1 lemon
small handful of fresh mint leaves,
  roughly chopped
small bunch of fresh coriander
  (cilantro), roughly chopped
sea salt and ground black pepper

Serves 4

NUTRITIONAL INFORMATION: Energy 97kcal/405.46 kJ; Protein 2g; Carbohydrate 4g, of which sugars 4g; Fat 8g, of which saturates 1g; Cholesterol 0mg; Calcium 33mg; Fibre 1g; Sodium 350mg

1 Place the peppers on a hot griddle, or directly over a gas flame or charcoal grill, turning until the skin is evenly charred. Leave them in a plastic bag for a few minutes to sweat, then hold each one under cold running water and peel off the skin. Remove the stalks and seeds, dice the flesh and place in a bowl.

2 Pit the black and green olives and slice in half lengthways. Add the halves to the bowl with the chopped peppers.

3 Add the tomatoes, spring onions and herbs and pour in the oil and lemon juice. Season and mix. Serve on its own, or with crisped pitta bread. Leftovers will keep in the refrigerator.

APPLE AND LEAF LIFT-OFF

68 Calories

This refreshing blend of apple, fresh green leaves and lime juice will give you over a third of your daily vitamin C needs, as well as an instant energy boost.

85g/3oz apple
sprigs of fresh coriander (cilantro)
25g/1oz watercress
15ml/1 tbsp lime juice

Serves 2

NUTRITIONAL INFORMATION: Energy 68kcal/284.24 kJ; Protein 1g; Carbohydrate 16g, of which sugars 16g; Fat Trace, of which saturates 0g; Cholesterol 0mg; Calcium 38mg; Fibre 2g; Sodium 10mg

1 Quarter the apple. Using a juice extractor, juice the apple, coriander sprigs and watercress.

2 Add the lime juice to the fruit and herb mixture and stir. Pour into a tall glass and serve immediately.

FENNEL FUSION

39 Calories

This hefty combination of raw vegetables and apple makes a surprisingly delicious juice. The cleansing tastes of lemon and fennel lift the red cabbage.

75g/3oz red cabbage
75g/3oz fennel bulb
115g/4oz apple
15ml/1 tbsp lemon juice

Serves 2

NUTRITIONAL INFORMATION: Energy 39kcal/163.02kJ; Protein 1g; Carbohydrate 9g, of which sugars 9g; Fat Trace, of which saturates 0g; Cholesterol 0mg; Calcium 72mg; Fibre 3g; Sodium 9mg

1 Roughly slice the cabbage, fennel and apple. Using a juice extractor, juice the vegetables and fruit.

2 Add the lemon juice to the juice mixture and stir. Pour into a glass and serve immediately.

Fasting tip The lemon will stop this juice discolouring, so it's a good option for making in the morning and taking with you to work or school for a low-calorie lunch.

SUGAR SNAP PEA JUICE

71 Calories

The sweetness of the peas and the melon intensifies when they are juiced and the fresh root ginger adds a warm edge to this mellow, cooling juice.

1cm/½in piece fresh root ginger, peeled
115g/4oz honeydew or Galia melon
115g/4oz sugar snap peas

Serves 1

NUTRITIONAL INFORMATION: Energy 71kcal/296.78kJ; Protein 5g; Carbohydrate 13g, of which sugars 10g; Fat Trace, of which saturates 0g; Cholesterol 0mg; Calcium 79mg; Fibre 2g; Sodium 41mg

1 Using a sharp knife, chop the ginger. Scoop out the seeds from the melon and cut it into wedges. Cut away the skin, then chop the flesh into chunks.

2 Push most of the sugar snap peas through a juicer, retaining a few, followed by most of the melon chunks and the ginger. Serve garnished with reserved melon chunks and podded peas.

CELERY SENSATION

38 Calories

Sticks of crunchy celery have one of the lowest calorie contents of all vegetables, so this is a particularly useful juice for fasting days.

3 celery sticks
15g/½oz rocket (arugula)
50g/2oz green grapes
crushed ice
salt and white pepper

Serves 1

NUTRITIONAL INFORMATION: Energy 38kcal/158.84kJ; Protein 1g; Carbohydrate 8g, of which sugars 8g; Fat Trace, of which saturates 0g; Cholesterol 0mg; Calcium 55mg; Fibre 1g; Sodium 396mg

1 Push two of the celery sticks through a juicer, followed by the rocket and the green grapes. Season to taste with a little salt and white pepper.

2 Put a leafy celery stick in a large glass to act as an edible swizzle stick and half-fill with crushed ice. Pour the juice over the ice and serve.

Fasting tip Adding some salt to low-calorie dishes on fasting days is a good idea; it makes up for the fact that the food is low on sugar and fat, and makes it more palatable.

CARROT AND CITRUS JUICE

85 Calories

This vibrant, intensely flavoured combination is packed with B-Carotene and vitamin C to boost the immune system. It is also low in calories.

6 clementines, scrubbed
200g/7oz carrots
salt

Serves 2

NUTRITIONAL INFORMATION: Energy 85kcal/355.3kJ; Protein 2g; Carbohydrate 20g, of which sugars 19g; Fat 1g, of which saturates 0g; Cholesterol 0mg; Calcium 66mg; Fibre 4g; Sodium 453mg

1 Quarter the clementines, still with their skin on, discarding any pips (seeds). Scrub the carrots and chop them into large chunks of more or less the same size.

2 Push the clementines through a juicer, then repeat the procedure with the carrots. Add salt to taste. Pour the juice into tall glasses and decorate with a wedge or slice of clementine.

GAZPACHO JUICE

42 Calories

Inspired by the classic Spanish soup, this fabulous juice looks and tastes delicious. Use the freshest, ripest ingredients for the best flavour. For picture, see page 47.

200g/7oz tomatoes, skinned
115g/4oz cucumber, roughly sliced
½ red (bell) pepper, seeded and cut
   into chunks
1 celery stick, chopped
1 spring onion (scallion), roughly
   chopped
fresh red chilli, to taste
juice of 1 lime
salt
a few sprigs of fresh coriander
   (cilantro) and ice cubes, to serve

Serves 2

NUTRITIONAL INFORMATION: Energy 42kcal/175.56kJ; Protein 3g; Carbohydrate 6g, of which sugars 6g; Fat 1g, of which saturates 0g; Cholesterol 0mg; Calcium 53mg; Fibre 2g; Sodium 426mg

1 Put the tomatoes, cucumber, red pepper, celery and spring onion in a food processor or blender. Remove and discard the seeds from the chilli and add to the other vegetables, along with the coriander.

2 Blend well until completely liquid, scraping the mixture down from the sides of the bowl if necessary.

3 Add the lime juice and a little salt to the juice and blend briefly to combine. Pour into glasses and add ice cubes and a few coriander leaves to serve.

RED ALERT JUICE

78 Calories

Beetroot, carrots and spinach all help maintain a healthy brain, while the addition of fresh orange juice will give you a natural vitamin boost in this low-calorie juice.

115g/4oz raw beetroot (beet)
55g/2oz carrot
1 small orange
25g/1oz spinach
salt and ground black pepper

Serves 2

NUTRITIONAL INFORMATION: Energy 78kcal/326.04kJ; Protein 7g; Carbohydrate 5g, of which sugars 5g; Fat 3g, of which saturates 0g; Cholesterol 8mg; Calcium 40mg; Fibre 2g; Sodium 86mg

1 Using a sharp knife, peel the beetroot and cut into wedges. Roughly chop the carrot, then cut away the skin from the orange and roughly slice the flesh.

2 Push the orange, beetroot and carrot pieces alternately through a juicer, then add the spinach, and season to taste with salt and pepper. Pour into glasses.

BASIL BLUSH

40 Calories

Most herbs don't really juice well, but basil is excellent, keeping its distinctive fresh fragrance. It makes the perfect partner for mild, refreshing cucumber.

115g/4oz cucumber, peeled
a few leaves of fresh basil
350g/12oz tomatoes
salt
basil sprigs, to decorate

Serves 2

NUTRITIONAL INFORMATION: Energy 40kcal/167.2kJ; Protein 2g; Carbohydrate 7g, of which sugars 7g; Fat 1g, of which saturates Trace; Cholesterol 0mg; Calcium 35mg; Fibre 2g; Sodium 413mg

1 Quarter the peeled cucumber lengthways. There's no need to remove the seeds. Push it through a juicer with the basil, then do the same with the tomatoes. Season with salt.

2 Divide the tomato, basil and cucumber juice between two short glasses and echo the herb flavour by serving with a torn basil leaf.

Variation Use a handful of rocket (arugula) or watercress if you don't have any fresh basil.

CREAMED COCONUT MACAROONS

54 Calories

Creamed coconut comes in a compressed block, which needs to be grated. It adds a rich creaminess to these lovely little macaroons.

50g/2oz creamed coconut, chilled and grated
2 large (US extra large) egg whites
90g/3½oz/½ cup caster (superfine) sugar
75g/3oz/1 cup desiccated (dry unsweetened shredded) coconut

Makes 18

Fasting tip Use a heat-stable, low-calorie sugar to reduce calories, check the packet for details.

NUTRITIONAL INFORMATION: Energy 54kcal/226kJ; Protein 1g; Carbohydrate 6g, of which sugars 6g; Fat 3g, of which saturates 3g; Cholesterol 0mg; Calcium 2mg; Fibre 1g; Sodium 8mg

1 Preheat the oven to 180°C/350°F/Gas 4. Line a large baking sheet with baking parchment. Use an electric beater to whisk the egg whites in a large bowl until stiff. Whisk in the sugar, a little at a time, to make a stiff and glossy meringue. Fold in the grated creamed coconut, and the desiccated coconut, using a large, metal spoon.

2 Place spoonfuls of the mixture, spaced slightly apart, on the baking sheet. Bake for 15–20 minutes, until slightly risen and golden. Leave to cool, then transfer to an airtight container.

ALMOND AND CARDAMOM MACAROONS

46 Calories

One of these tiny but wonderful macaroons, scented with cardamom, may be the perfect end to your fasting day to help curb any sweet cravings.

1.5ml/¼ tsp cardamom seeds
4 large (US extra large) egg whites
250g/9oz/generous 2 cups icing (confectioners') sugar
115g/4oz/1 cup ground almonds
100ml/4fl oz/1 cup Greek yogurt
100g/4oz/scant 1 cup blueberries

Makes 20

NUTRITIONAL INFORMATION: Energy 46kcal/192kJ; Protein 1g; Carbohydrate 7g, of which sugars 7g; Fat 2g, of which saturates Trace; Cholesterol 0mg; Calcium 11mg; Fibre Trace; Sodium 9mg

1 Preheat the oven to 200°C/400°F/Gas 6 and line two large baking sheets with baking parchment. Grind the cardamom seeds finely using a mortar and pestle.

2 Put the egg whites into a bowl and whisk until they form stiff peaks. Using a metal spoon, gently fold in the icing sugar a little at a time. Fold in the almonds and cardamom.

3 Using a teaspoon, spoon the mixture on to the baking parchment, about 5cm/2in apart. Bake for 8–10 minutes, or until golden. Leave the macaroons to cool on the tray.

4 Slightly crush the berries and stir in to the yogurt, and use the mixture to sandwich pairs of macaroons together to serve.

BAKED APPLES WITH MINCEMEAT

111 Calories

These baked apples are stuffed with mincemeat, rather than butter and sugar, to give a lower calorie count. Serve with a drizzle of natural yogurt.

4 medium-sized cooking apples
40ml/8 tsp mincemeat
115g/4oz yogurt, to serve

Serves 4

NUTRITIONAL INFORMATION: Energy 111kcal/464kJ; Protein 2g; Carbohydrate 25g, of which sugars 25g; Fat 1g, of which saturates Trace; Cholesterol 2mg; Calcium 64mg; Fibre 3g; Sodium 30mg

1 Preheat the oven to 180°C/350°F/Gas 4. With a small sharp knife, remove the cores from the apples.

2 Run a sharp knife around the middle of each apple, cutting through the skin but not deep into the flesh. Stand the apples in an ovenproof dish.

3 Fill the hollow centres of the apples with 2 teaspoons each of mincemeat. Add 60ml/4 tbsp water to the dish. Bake for about 45 minutes until soft throughout, and serve with yogurt.

POACHED PEARS

89 Calories

Delicately spiced, these pears can be served warm, or chilled. If you have enough calories to spare, serve with 15ml/1 tbsp low-fat crème fraîche (24 calories).

75g/3oz/⅓ cup sugar
grated rind and juice of 1 lemon
2.5ml/½ tsp ground ginger
1 small cinnamon stick
2 whole cloves
4 firm pears

Serves 4

NUTRITIONAL INFORMATION: Energy 89kcal/372kJ; Protein 1g; Carbohydrate 23g, of which sugars 23g; Fat Trace, of which saturates 0g; Cholesterol 0mg; Calcium 19mg; Fibre 4g; Sodium 5mg

1 Put the sugar in a pan with 200ml/7fl oz/scant 1 cup water, the lemon rind and juice, ginger and spices. Heat, stirring, until the sugar has dissolved.

2 Peel the pears, cut them in half lengthways and remove their cores. Add the pear halves to the pan and bring just to the boil.

3 Cover and simmer very gently for about 5 minutes or until the pears are tender, turning them over in the syrup occasionally during cooking. Add a little more water if needed.

4 Remove from the heat and leave to cool in the syrup. Serve the pears, without any added syrup, at room temperature or chilled.

COFFEE GRANITA

73 Calories

Granitas are very low in calories and are completely fat-free. A small helping is a good way of finishing a meal with a little sweetness, without ruining a fasting day.

75ml/5 tbsp good quality ground filter coffee
1 litre/1¾ pints/4 cups boiling water
75g/3oz/⅓ cup sugar

Serves 4

NUTRITIONAL INFORMATION: Energy 73kcal/305kJ; Protein 0g; Carbohydrate 20g, of which sugars 20g; Fat 0g, of which saturates 0g; Cholesterol 0mg; Calcium 2mg; Fibre 0g; Sodium 1mg

1 Spoon the coffee into a cafetière (press pot), pour on the boiling water and leave to stand for 5 minutes. Plunge the cafetière and pour the coffee into a large plastic container, to a maximum depth of 2.5cm/1in. Add the sugar and stir until it has dissolved. Leave the mixture to cool.

2 Cover and freeze for 2 hours until the mixture round the sides of the container is starting to become mushy. Using a fork, break up the ice crystals and mash finely. Return to the freezer for 2 hours more, beating every 30 minutes until the ice becomes fine, even crystals. After the final beating return to the freezer. To serve, spoon the granita into glass dishes.

RASPBERRY GRANITA

80 Calories

This vibrant red granita is a perfect low-calorie dessert for fasting days; on other days serve it with whole berries and crème fraîche.

55g/2oz/¼ cup sugar
500g/1¼ lb/3½ cups raspberries

Serves 4

NUTRITIONAL INFORMATION: Energy 80kcal/334kJ; Protein 2g; Carbohydrate 19g, of which sugars 19g; Fat Trace, of which saturates 0g; Cholesterol 0mg; Calcium 32mg; Fibre 8g; Sodium 4mg

1 Tip the sugar and 300ml/½ pint/1¼ cups water into a large pan and bring to the boil, stirring until the sugar has dissolved. Pour the sugar syrup into a bowl, leave to cool, then chill. Purée the raspberries in a food processor or in batches in a blender.

2 Press the purée through a sieve (strainer) into a bowl and discard the seeds. Stir in the syrup and add 1 litre/1¾ pints/ 4 cups water. Pour into a large plastic container to a depth no more than 2.5cm/1in. Cover and freeze for 2 hours.

3 Using a fork, break up the ice crystals and mash finely. Return to the freezer for 2 hours, beating every 30 minutes until the ice forms fine, even crystals. Serve in glasses.

GINGER GRANITA

80 Calories

A full-bloodied granita, this is a fiery dessert that can be served as a palate-cleanser for a sophisticated dinner party, as well as a great fasting day treat.

75g/3oz/⅓ cup sugar
75g/3oz root ginger, peeled and
    chopped finely
ground cinnamon, to decorate

Serves 4

NUTRITIONAL INFORMATION: Energy 80kcal/334kJ; Protein Trace; Carbohydrate 21g, of which sugars 20g; Fat 0g, of which saturates 0g; Cholesterol 0mg; Calcium 5mg; Fibre 0g; Sodium 3mg

1 Put the sugar and 1 litre/1¾ pints/4 cups water into a pan. Bring to the boil, stirring until the sugar has dissolved. Remove from the heat and stir the ginger into the hot syrup. Leave for at least 1 hour to infuse, then pour into a bowl and chill.

2 Strain the chilled syrup into a large, shallow plastic container, to a depth no more than 2.5cm/1in. Cover and freeze for 2 hours then break up the ice crystals and mash finely with a fork.

3 Return the granita to the freezer for 2 hours more, beating every 30 minutes. Serve in glasses, dusted with cinnamon.

SOUPS

Nourishing and sustaining, soups are such a useful food on fasting days. Soup satisfies brain and tummy hunger quickly, curbing the desire for further intake, and can be bulked out with noodles or croutons for people who are eating with you. Most soups are easy to store, either in the freezer or refrigerator, with the exception of fish soups, as the tender flesh may toughen. Fill your cupboard with soup staples such as high-quality stock, miso, dashi-no-moto and wakami, from Oriental food stores. Japanese zero-calorie noodles and rice, made from the fibre-rich Konjac plant, are a good way to add bulk.

◀ Haricot bean soup.
▼ Miso soup.

CHILLI & LIME FISH SOUP

145 Calories

This Latin American fish soup has a clean, fresh taste from the lime, and a gentle kick of chilli. A clear soup, it is very low in calories; double the portion if you've saved enough calories until the end of the day.

2 litres/3½ pints/8 cups water
2 garlic cloves, very finely chopped
1 small red onion, finely chopped
2 spring onions (scallions), finely
  chopped
1 red chilli, seeded and finely
  chopped
30ml/2 tbsp fresh parsley, chopped
2 medium white fish, such as sea
  bass, about 1kg/2¼lb total
  weight, cleaned and gutted
salt and ground black pepper
1 lime, sliced, to serve

Serves 6

NUTRITIONAL INFORMATION: Energy 145kcal/606kJ; Protein 31g; Carbohydrate 1g, of which sugars 1g; Fat 2g, of which saturates 1g; Cholesterol 0mg; Calcium 63mg; Fibre 1g; Sodium 164mg

1 Bring the water to the boil in a large pan with the garlic, red onion, and half the spring onion, chilli and parsley. When it bubbles, lay the fish in the pan. Season. Return to the boil, reduce the heat, cover and simmer for 10 minutes.

2 Lift out the fish and leave the soup simmering, uncovered, for a further 15–20 minutes to reduce and concentrate the flavour. Meanwhile, remove the heads and tails from the fish, take off the fillets and divide into individual portions. Keep warm.

3 Strain the soup and adjust the seasoning to taste. Divide the pieces of fish among hot bowls, pour over the stock, garnish with the reserved spring onion, chilli and parsley, and serve with slices of lime.

FISH SOUP WITH ORANGE

220 Calories

This generous, tangy Spanish soup, flavoured with Seville oranges, is great for a weekend lunch; non-fasters can eat larger helpings with crusty bread and butter. You could also add a few more potatoes to the recipe, but avoid them in your portion.

1kg/2¼lb small hake or whiting, whole but cleaned
1.2 litres/2 pints/5 cups water
15ml/1 tbsp olive oil
1 large onion, finely chopped
5 garlic cloves, unpeeled
1 tomato, peeled, seeded and chopped
4 baby new potatoes, cut into rounds
juice of 4 bitter oranges or 4 sweet oranges and 2 lemons
5ml/1 tsp paprika
salt and ground black pepper
30ml/2 tbsp fresh parsley, finely chopped, to garnish

Serves 6

NUTRITIONAL INFORMATION: Energy 220kcal/920kJ; Protein 31g; Carbohydrate 10g, of which sugars 5g; Fat 7g, of which saturates 1g; Cholesterol 38mg; Calcium 49mg; Fibre 1g; Sodium 176mg

1 Fillet the fish and cut each fillet into three, reserving all the trimmings. Put the fillets on a plate, salt lightly and chill.

2 Put the trimmings in a pan, add the water and a spiral of orange rind. Bring to a simmer, skim, then cover and cook gently for 30 minutes.

3 Strain in the hot fish stock (adding the orange spiral as well if you wish) and bring back to the boil. Add the onion, garlic, tomato and potatoes and cook for about 10–15 minutes.

4 Add the fish pieces to the soup, a few at a time, without letting it go off the boil. Cook for about 5–10 minutes. Add the squeezed citrus juices, and the paprika, with salt and pepper to taste. Serve in bowls, garnished with a little parsley.

CLEAR COD SOUP

This is a fragrantly clear soup, which is high in taste and protein and low in calories. When cooked, the long stalks of enoki mushrooms look like noodles.

25g/1oz dried anchovies
225g/8oz daikon (white radish), peeled and diced
600g/1lb 6oz cod fillet, skinned and cut into wide strips
2 garlic cloves, crushed
2 spring onions (scallions), sliced
½ leek, finely sliced
175g/7oz firm tofu, cubed
50g/2oz enoki mushrooms
50g/2oz watercress
½ hot red chilli, seeded and sliced
salt and ground black pepper

Serves 4

NUTRITIONAL INFORMATION: Energy 164kcal/686kJ; Protein 32g; Carbohydrate 2g, of which sugars 1g; Fat 3g of which saturates 1g; Cholesterol 73mg; Calcium 196mg; Fibre 1g; Sodium 350mg

1 Bring 1.5 litres/2½ pints/6¼ cups water to the boil in large pan and add the dried anchovies. Boil for 10 minutes over a high heat, then use a slotted spoon to remove the anchovies. Discard the anchovies.

2 Add the daikon to the stock. Simmer the soup for about 4 minutes, until the daikon is just cooked. Stir in the fish, garlic, spring onions and leek. Add the tofu and simmer for a further 10 minutes, but do not stir or the tofu will break up.

3 Add the enoki mushrooms, watercress, chilli and salt. Increase the heat and boil for 2 minutes. Add pepper and serve.

SPINACH AND CLAM SOUP

148 Calories

This deep and intense soup combines beef with clams, and gets its flavour from doenjang soya bean paste. If you can't find this, use miso instead.

9 clams
90g/3½oz spinach
2 spring onions (scallions)
40g/1½oz/scant ¼ cup minced
   (ground) beef
15ml/1 tbsp doenjang soya bean
   paste
1 clove garlic, crushed
salt

Serves 2

NUTRITIONAL INFORMATION: Energy 148kcal/619kJ; Protein 18g; Carbohydrate 2g, of which sugars 1g; Fat 7g of which saturates 2g; Cholesterol 12mg; Calcium 157mg; Fibre 1g; Sodium 174mg

1 Scrub the clams in cold water, and rinse the spinach. Cut the spring onions lengthways and then into 5cm/2in strips. Stir the beef and the soya bean paste in a large non-stick pan, over a medium heat, until they are cooked.

2 Pour in 750ml/1¼ pints/3 cups water and bring to the boil. Add the clams and spinach and simmer for 5 minutes. When the clams have opened, add the spring onions and garlic. Discard any closed clams. Season and serve.

MISO SOUP

Asian soups are great for fasting days, they are quick to prepare, nutritious, and often very low in calories. Wakame, Japanese seaweed, is widely available.

5ml/1 tsp dried wakame
115g/4oz fresh soft tofu
200ml/7fl oz/1 cup water and
   5ml/1 tsp dashi-no-moto
10ml/2 tsp miso
2 spring onions (scallions), finely
   sliced
black pepper

Serves 2

NUTRITIONAL INFORMATION: Energy 82kcal/343kJ; Protein 9g; Carbohydrate 2g, of which sugars 1g; Fat 4g of which saturates 1g; Cholesterol 0mg; Calcium 227mg; Fibre 1g; Sodium 768mg

1 Soak the wakame in a large bowl of cold water for 15 minutes. Drain and chop into stamp-size pieces. Cut the tofu into cubes.

2 Bring the dashi stock to the boil. Put the miso in a small cup and mix with 60ml/4 tbsp hot stock from the pan. Reduce the heat to low and add two-thirds of the miso into the stock. Taste the soup and add more miso if required. Add the wakame and the tofu and increase the heat.

3 Just before the soup comes to the boil again, add the spring onions and remove from the heat. Do not boil. Serve sprinkled with black pepper.

CLEAR SOUP WITH SEAFOOD STICKS

This pretty soup, with chive-tied seafood sticks, is quick and easy to make and so low in calories that you could even make it as an appetizer, followed by a stir-fry.

4 chives
sprigs of fresh coriander (cilantro)
4 seafood sticks
200ml/7fl oz/1 cup water and
   2.5ml/½ tsp dashi-no-moto
10ml/2 tsp soy sauce
salt, to taste
grated rind of lemon

Serves 2

NUTRITIONAL INFORMATION: Energy 34kcal/142kJ; Protein 4g; Carbohydrate 4g, of which sugars Trace; Fat Trace, of which saturates 0g; Cholesterol 6mg; Calcium 4mg; Fibre 0g; Sodium 712mg

1 Choose chives that are at least 10cm/4in in length and tie one around the middle of each seafood stick with a sprig of coriander. Place two tied seafood sticks in each soup bowl.

2 Heat the stock in a pan and bring to the boil. Add soy sauce and salt to taste. Pour the stock gently over the seafood sticks. Serve, sprinkled with grated lemon rind.

SOUP WITH PORK AND VEGETABLES 109 Calories

This Chinese soup is more substantial, and therefore ideal for a meal at the end of the day. Adding 15g/¹⁄₂oz noodles at the end of cooking will add 64 calories.

55g/2oz daikon (white radish)
4 fresh shiitake mushrooms
5ml/1 tsp each vegetable oil and
   sesame oil
110g/4oz lean pork fillet, cut into
   very thin strips
1 small parsnip, thinly sliced
10ml/2 tsp miso
5ml/1 tsp dashi-no-moto
115g/4oz firm tofu, diced
2 spring onions (scallions),
   chopped
5ml/1 tsp sesame seeds

Serves 4

NUTRITIONAL INFORMATION: Energy 109kcal/456kJ; Protein 11g; Carbohydrate 3g, of which sugars 1g; Fat 6g of which saturates 1g; Cholesterol 17mg; Calcium 125mg; Fibre 1g; Sodium 325mg

1 Peel the daikon and parsnip and cut into 1.5cm/²⁄₃in discs. Cut the discs into cubes. Slice the shiitake mushrooms.

2 Heat the oils in a heavy pan and stir-fry the pork. When cooked add the parsnip, daikon and mushrooms, and stir in the miso. Add 300ml/¹⁄₂ pint/1 cup water and the dashi-no-moto and bring to the boil. Drop in the tofu, reduce the heat, cover, and simmer for 15 minutes.

3 Taste and add more seasoning if required. Add the spring onion and serve sprinkled with sesame seeds.

DAIKON AND BEEF SOUP 85 Calories

The smoky flavours of the beef are complemented by the sweet tang of daikon in this mild soup. Great for lunch, or double the portions to serve as an evening meal.

115g/4oz daikon (white radish)
50g/2oz lean beef fillet
10ml/2 tsp vegetable oil
¹⁄₂ leek, sliced
15ml/1 tbsp light soy sauce
sliced green chilli, to garnish

Serves 2

NUTRITIONAL INFORMATION: Energy 85kcal/355kJ; Protein 6g Carbohydrate 3g, of which sugars 3g; Fat 5g, of which saturates 1g; Cholesterol 0mg; Calcium 22mg; Fibre 1g; Sodium 546mg

1 Peel and slice the white radish, and cut the pieces into 2cm/³⁄₄in squares. Roughly chop the beef into bite-size cubes.

2 Heat the oil in a large pan, and stir-fry the beef until tender and golden brown. Add the daikon, and briefly stir-fry.

3 Add 300ml/¹⁄₂ pint/1 cup water to the pan. Bring to the boil, cover and simmer for 7 minutes. Add the sliced leek and soy sauce. Simmer for a further 2 minutes to wilt the leek.

4 Season to taste, garnish with slices of green chilli, and serve.

CHICKEN SOUP

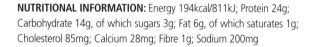 194 Calories

This saffron-scented soup comes from the Lebanon, and is lighter and less calorific than most chicken soups. The recipe requires only the white meat, which is half the fat and lower in calories than the dark meat. A great family lunch, simply add some more cooked vermicelli to larger helpings of soup for non-fasting diners.

2 celery stalks, with leaves, roughly chopped
2 medium-sized carrots, peeled and roughly chopped
1 onion, roughly chopped
1 lean, organic chicken, about 1.5kg/3¼lb, cleaned and trimmed
small bunch of parsley, roughly chopped
6 peppercorns
6 allspice berries
generous pinch of saffron fronds
115g/4oz/1 cup vermicelli, broken into pieces
sea salt and ground black pepper
small bunch of fresh parsley or mint, finely chopped, to garnish

Serves 8

NUTRITIONAL INFORMATION: Energy 194kcal/811kJ; Protein 24g; Carbohydrate 14g, of which sugars 3g; Fat 6g, of which saturates 1g; Cholesterol 85mg; Calcium 28mg; Fibre 1g; Sodium 200mg

1 To make the stock, place all the chopped vegetables in a large pan. Put the chicken on top of the vegetables, and add the parsley, peppercorns and allspice berries. Pour in just enough water to cover the chicken.

2 Bring the water to the boil, then reduce the heat, cover the pan and simmer gently for about 1½ hours, until the chicken is practically falling off the bones.

3 Lift the chicken out of the pan and set aside. Strain the stock into a fresh pan and discard the vegetables and spices.

4 When the chicken is cool enough to handle, pull the meat off the carcass and measure 115g/4oz of white meat per person. Discard the bones, and reserve the dark meat for another dish. Use your fingers to tear the breast meat into thin strips, cover and keep warm.

5 Reheat the broth and stir in the saffron fronds. Bring the broth to the boil and add the vermicelli. Reduce the heat and boil gently for about 5 minutes until the vermicelli is cooked.

6 Add the chicken strips to the soup and heat through. Check the seasoning and add salt and pepper to taste. Pour the hot soup into individual bowls and sprinkle with a little parsley or mint before serving.

Cook's tip If you are making the soup in advance, stop preparation at step 5, and add the vermicelli and cooked chicken when you are reheating the soup.

Fasting tip Replace the vermicelli with zero-calorie noodles, if you wish; this would reduce each portion to 144 calories.

VELVETY PUMPKIN SOUP

125 Calories

Pumpkin flesh makes a beautifully smooth, golden-coloured soup, and this is a great recipe for freezing in portions and heating up as you need it. The addition of a spoonful of rice, if you have calories to spare, makes a balanced lunch.

1.1kg/2lb 7oz pumpkin
750ml/1¼ pints/3 cups chicken
   stock
750ml/1¼ pints/3 cups skimmed
   milk
salt and ground black pepper
ground cinnamon, to serve
75g/3oz/½ cup cooked rice to
   serve, (optional)

Serves 4

Fasting tip Adding 75g/3oz
cooked rice shared between
four portions increases the
calorie count to 137kcals.

NUTRITIONAL INFORMATION: Energy 125kcal/523kJ; Protein 9g;
Carbohydrate 20g, of which sugars 13g; Fat 1g, of which saturates Trace;
Cholesterol 6mg; Calcium 312mg; Fibre 3g; Sodium 687mg

1 Remove the seeds or fibre from the pumpkin, cut off the peel
and chop the flesh. Put the prepared pumpkin in a pan and add
the stock, milk and seasoning.

2 Bring to the boil, then reduce the heat and simmer for about
20 minutes, or until the pumpkin is tender. Drain the pumpkin,
reserving the liquid, and purée it in a food processor, then
return it to the pan with the stock.

3 Bring the soup back to a near boil again. Check the
seasoning, and pour into bowls. Dust with cinnamon and add a
spoonful of cooked rice, if using.

YELLOW PEA AND LENTIL SOUP

183 Calories

Pulses are a good fast day food, as a small portion can be very sustaining. Yellow peas are rich and buttery, and red lentils have a sweet, nutty flavour – together they provide a hearty, high-protein dish for a fast day supper.

50g/2oz lean smoked bacon, cut into cubes
5ml/1 tsp vegetable oil
1 onion, finely chopped
150g/5oz/generous ⅔ cup dried yellow peas
115g/4oz/½ cup red lentils
5ml/1 tsp paprika
2.5ml/½ tsp cumin
1.5 litres/2½ pints/6¼ cups chicken stock
fresh parsley sprigs, finely chopped
salt and ground black pepper

Serves 6

NUTRITIONAL INFORMATION: Energy 183kcal/765kJ; Protein 13g; Carbohydrate 26g, of which sugars 3g; Fat 4g, of which saturates 1g; Cholesterol 5mg; Calcium 40mg; Fibre 5g; Sodium 569mg

1 Put the bacon in a large pan over medium-high heat with a little water. Stir and cook for 2–3 minutes, or until golden. Add the oil and onion and continue cooking over low heat for 3 minutes until the onion is translucent.

2 Add the yellow peas and red lentils, and stir to coat well. Season to taste, add the paprika and cumin, and then the stock.

3 Simmer over medium heat for 1 hour. Check the seasoning, and serve sprinkled with the parsley.

HARICOT BEAN SOUP

213 Calories

This hearty and substantial soup is full of flavour, with nutritious and low-GI beans. It is perfect for making in advance, to come home to after a day of fasting.

10ml/2 tsp olive oil
2 ripe tomatoes, chopped
3 garlic cloves, crushed
1 onion, finely chopped
2 celery sticks, finely chopped
1 carrot, finely chopped
225g/8oz/1 cup dried haricot
   (navy) beans, soaked overnight,
   drained and rinsed
5ml/1 tsp paprika
2.5ml/½ tsp cayenne pepper
1.2 litres/2 pints/5 cups chicken
   stock
1 small bunch fresh parsley, leaves
   finely chopped
salt and ground black pepper

Serves 4

NUTRITIONAL INFORMATION: Energy 213kcal/890kJ; Protein 14g; Carbohydrate 33g, of which sugars 5g; Fat 4g, of which saturates 1g; Cholesterol 0mg; Calcium 126mg; Fibre 13g; Sodium 530mg

1 Put the oil in a large pan over medium heat. Add the tomatoes, garlic, onion, celery and carrot.

2 Sauté the contents of the pan for 5 minutes, stirring constantly. Season to taste with salt and pepper. Add the drained beans, paprika and cayenne pepper.

3 Pour the stock into the pan, and simmer for 1½ hours, or until the beans are soft. Add the parsley and serve hot.

Fasting tip This soup freezes well, so divide what is left into fast-day sized portions.

BUTTER BEAN SOUP

141 Calories

This is a simple soup, which can be cooked in a matter of minutes. It gets its flavour from pesto and sun-dried tomato purée, which give it an Italian taste.

900ml/1½ pints/3¾ cups stock
2 x 400g/14oz cans butter (lima)
  beans, drained and rinsed
30ml/2 tbsp sun-dried tomato
  purée (paste)
30ml/2 tbsp pesto

Serves 4

NUTRITIONAL INFORMATION: Energy 141kcal/589kJ; Protein 9g; Carbohydrate 17g, of which sugars 3g; Fat 5g, of which saturates 1g; Cholesterol 3mg; Calcium 63mg; Fibre 5g; Sodium 968mg

1 Put the stock in a pan with the butter beans and bring just to the boil. Reduce the heat and stir in the tomato purée and pesto. Cook gently for 5 minutes.

2 Transfer six ladlefuls of the soup to a blender or food processor, scooping up plenty of the beans. Process until smooth, then return the purée to the pan. Reheat gently, check the seasoning, and serve.

LEEK AND OATMEAL SOUP

117 Calories

This traditional soup is an Irish recipe, and is beautifully easy to make. For any non-fasting people who are eating with you, it can be served with a swirl of cream.

1.2 litres/2 pints/5 cups chicken
  stock and skimmed milk, mixed
30ml/2 tbsp medium oatmeal
6 large leeks, washed and sliced
sea salt and ground black pepper
pinch of ground mace

Serves 4

NUTRITIONAL INFORMATION: Energy 117kcal/489kJ; Protein 9g; Carbohydrate 17g, of which sugars 10g; Fat 2g, of which saturates Trace; Cholesterol 6mg; Calcium 239mg; Fibre 4g; Sodium 480mg

1 Bring the stock and milk mixture to the boil over a medium heat and sprinkle in the oatmeal. Stir well to prevent lumps forming, and then simmer gently.

2 Cook the leeks, covered, in a splash of water until softened, then add them to the stock mixture. Simmer for a further 15–20 minutes, until the oatmeal is cooked. Extra stock can be added if the soup is too thick.

3 Season with salt, pepper and mace, stir in the parsley and serve in warmed bowls.

Variation Add some chopped parsley, to serve, if you wish.

COUNTRY VEGETABLE SOUP

149 Calories

This is a healthy soup, packed with vegetables. If you make it in advance and freeze in portion-sized batches for fast days, reheat gently and don't let it boil.

15ml/1 tbsp oil and 25g/1oz butter
2 medium onions, finely chopped
4 medium carrots, sliced
2 celery sticks, sliced
2 leeks, trimmed and sliced
1 potato, diced
1 small parsnip, diced
1 garlic clove, crushed
1 litre/2 pints/4 cups stock
150ml/¼ pint/⅔ cup skimmed milk
25g/1oz/4 tbsp cornflour
   (cornstarch)
55g/2oz frozen peas
30ml/2 tbsp fresh parsley, chopped
salt and ground black pepper

Serves 6

NUTRITIONAL INFORMATION: Energy 149kcal/623kJ; Protein 4g; Carbohydrate 20g, of which sugars 9g; Fat 7g, of which saturates 3g; Cholesterol 10mg; Calcium 81mg; Fibre 4g; Sodium 284mg

1 Heat the oil and butter in a large pan and add the onions, carrots and celery. Cook over a medium heat for 5–10 minutes, stirring occasionally, until soft and just beginning to turn golden brown. Stir in the leeks, potato, parsnip and garlic.

2 Add the stock to the pan and stir into the vegetables. Bring the mixture slowly to the boil, cover and simmer gently for 20–30 minutes until all the vegetables are soft.

3 Whisk the milk into the cornflour, making a paste. Stir into the vegetables. Add the frozen peas. Bring to the boil and simmer for 5 minutes. Adjust the seasoning, stir in the parsley and serve.

CELERY SOUP WITH STILTON

118 Calories

Stilton – like any cheese – is high in fat, but you only need a very small amount for its hefty flavour to add richness and taste to this soup.

15ml/1 tbsp vegetable oil
1 large onion, finely chopped
1 medium potato, cut into small
  cubes
1 whole head of celery, sliced
900ml/1½ pints/3¾ cups vegetable
  or chicken stock
75g/3oz Stilton cheese, crumbled
150ml/¼ pint/⅔ cup skimmed milk
salt and ground black pepper

Serves 6

NUTRITIONAL INFORMATION: Energy 118kcal/493kJ; Protein 5g; Carbohydrate 10g, of which sugars 4g; Fat 7g, of which saturates 3g; Cholesterol 12mg; Calcium 94mg; Fibre 2g; Sodium 355mg

1 Heat the oil in a large pan and add the onion. Cook over a medium heat for 5 minutes, stirring, until soft but not browned.

2 Stir in the potato and celery and cook for a further 5 minutes. Add the stock, bring to the boil, then cover and simmer gently for about 30 minutes, until all the vegetables are very soft.

3 Process or blend three-quarters of the mixture until smooth, then return to the pan. Bring the soup just to the boil and season to taste. Remove from the heat and stir in the cheese, reserving a little for serving. Add the milk and reheat without boiling. Serve topped with the reserved cheese.

SPICED PARSNIP AND APPLE SOUP 139 Calories

With less starch than potato, and therefore lower in calories, parsnips are still a
hearty and filling root vegetable. This is a sustaining soup, lightened with the apple.

12g/½oz butter
1 medium onion, finely chopped
1 garlic clove, finely chopped
350g/12oz parsnips, peeled and
    thinly sliced
5ml/1 tsp curry paste
100ml/3½fl oz/½ cup apple juice
1 litre/2 pints/4 cups vegetable
    stock
150ml/¼ pint/⅔ cup skimmed milk
salt and ground black pepper
natural (plain) yogurt, to serve
fresh parsley, chopped, to serve

Serves 4

NUTRITIONAL INFORMATION: Energy 139kcal/581kJ; Protein 4g;
Carbohydrate 22g, of which sugars 15g; Fat 4g, of which saturates 2g;
Cholesterol 8mg; Calcium 112mg; Fibre 4g; Sodium 491mg

1 Melt the butter in a large pan and add the onion, garlic and
parsnips. Cook gently, without browning, for about 10 minutes,
stirring often. Stir in the curry paste and cook for 1 minute.

2 Add the juice and stock, bring to the boil, cover and simmer
gently for about 20 minutes until the parsnips are soft. Process
or blend the mixture until smooth and return it to the pan.

3 Add the milk and season to taste with salt and pepper.
Reheat the soup gently and serve, top each portion with
5ml/1 tsp of yogurt and a sprinkling of herbs.

BORSCHT

There are many recipes for this Russian classic. This version has been tweaked to reduce the calories. Non-fasting diners can top their portion with sour cream.

12g/½oz butter
15ml/1 tbsp caraway seeds, plus
   extra for sprinkling
400g/14oz raw beetroot (beets),
   peeled and grated
250g/9oz red cabbage, shredded
1 large cooking apple, grated
15ml/1 tbsp red wine vinegar
1 medium carrot, grated
1 bay leaf
1 garlic clove
1 litre/2 pints/4 cups chicken stock
salt and ground black pepper
1 hard-boiled egg, chopped
natural (plain) yogurt, to serve

Serves 4

NUTRITIONAL INFORMATION: Energy 130kcal/543kJ; Protein 7g; Carbohydate 14g, of which sugars 13g; Fat 6g, of which saturates 2g; Cholesterol 84mg; Calcium 121mg; Fibre 5g; Sodium 464mg

1 Heat the butter in a large, heavy pan over a medium heat. When melted, add the caraway seeds and beetroot, and stir to coat in the butter. Season to taste.

2 Add the cabbage and apple to the pan, then the vinegar, carrots, bay leaf and garlic, and pour in the chicken stock. Cover and simmer gently for 2 hours, adding a little water if the liquid reduces too much.

3 Serve the borscht topped with the chopped hard-boiled egg, 5ml/1 tsp yogurt per serving, and a sprinkling of caraway seeds.

FISH & MEAT

This chapter has plenty of ideas for protein-rich fasting day dishes. An essential macronutrient, protein empties from the stomach more slowly relative to carbohydrates, fruit or vegetables, so is useful for keeping us feeling fuller for longer. Too much, however, will contribute to extra calories and slow down weight loss, but these recipes offer a careful balance. The fish and seafood recipes offer valuable nutrients such as omega-3 fats, while the meat recipes, using vibrant flavours and tastes, will tempt the senses as well as satisfy the appetite.

◀ Grilled hake with lemon and chilli.
▼ Yellow chicken curry.

MARINATED SASHIMI-STYLE TUNA

111 Calories

These little cubes of tuna are marinated for just 5 minutes in a delicious Japanese-style wasabi mixture that partially 'cooks' the fish. Use the freshest tuna possible.

150g/5oz very fresh tuna, skinned
10ml/2 tsp wasabi paste
30ml/2 tbsp soy sauce
4 spring onions (scallions), green
  part only, finely chopped
2 shiso or basil leaves, cut into thin
  slivers lengthways

Serves 2

NUTRITIONAL INFORMATION: Energy 111kcal/464kJ; Protein 18g; Carbohydrate 2g, of which sugars 2g; Fat 4g, of which saturates 1g; Cholesterol 20mg; Calcium 25mg; Fibre 0g; Sodium 1072mg

1 Cut the tuna into 2cm/¾in cubes. Just 5–10 minutes before serving, blend the wasabi paste with the soy sauce in a bowl, then add the tuna and spring onions.

2 Mix well and leave to marinate for 5 minutes. Divide among two plates, and add a few slivers of shiso or basil leaves on top. Serve immediately.

CRAB MEAT IN VINEGAR

75 Calories

White crab meat is a rich and very satisfying protein, but is only 97 calories per 115g/4oz, so makes a good main ingredient in this tangy Asian-style seafood salad.

½ red (bell) pepper, seeded
115g/4oz cooked white crab meat
10ml/2 tsp rice vinegar
2.5ml/½ tsp sugar
5ml/1 tsp soy sauce
150g/5oz cucumber
salt

Serves 2

NUTRITIONAL INFORMATION: Energy 75kcal/314kJ; Protein 12g; Carbohydrate 6g, of which sugars 5g; Fat 1g, of which saturates 0g; Cholesterol 41mg; Calcium 86mg; Fibre 1g; Sodium 497mg

1 Slice the red pepper into thin strips. Sprinkle with a little salt and leave for about 15 minutes to soften slightly. Rinse and drain. Loosen the crab meat and mix it with the red pepper in a bowl. Cover, and chill in the refrigerator.

2 Combine the rice vinegar, sugar and soy sauce in a bowl.

3 Cut the piece of cucumber in half, lengthways. Scoop out any seeds with a teaspoon. Finely grate the cucumber with a fine-toothed grater. Drain in a fine-meshed sieve (strainer). Mix the cucumber with the vinegar mixture.

4 Divide the crab meat mixture between two bowls, then pile half of the dressed cucumber in the centre of each. Serve immediately, before the cucumber loses its colour.

LIGHT AND FRAGRANT TIGER PRAWNS

175 Calories

The delicate flavour of fresh prawns goes really well with mild cucumber and fragrant dill in this simple dish, which is very quick and easy to prepare.

225g/8oz cucumber
15ml/1 tbsp olive oil
1 garlic clove, finely chopped
200g/7oz raw tiger prawns (jumbo
 shrimp), peeled with tails left on
10ml/1 tbsp chopped fresh dill
juice of ½ lemon
salt and ground black pepper

Serves 2

NUTRITIONAL INFORMATION: Energy 175kcal/732kJ; Protein 22g; Carbohydrate 2g, of which sugars 2g; Fat 8g, of which saturates 1g; Cholesterol 0mg; Calcium 197mg; Fibre 1g; Sodium 197mg

1 Peel the cucumber and slice in half lengthways. Using a small teaspoon, gently scoop out any seeds and discard. Cut the cucumber into sticks.

2 Heat a wok over a high heat, then add the oil. When hot, add the cucumber and garlic and stir-fry over a high heat for 2–3 minutes. Add the prawns to the wok and continue to stir-fry over a high heat for 3–4 minutes, or until the prawns turn pink and are just cooked through, then remove from the heat.

3 Add the fresh dill and lemon juice to the wok and toss to combine. Season well with salt and ground black pepper and serve while still sizzling hot.

PARCHMENT-WRAPPED PRAWNS

105 Calories

Wrapping these fragrantly-spiced prawns in baking parchment as they cook keeps them beautifully tender. Great for a fast day, with low-calorie content, you could also make these impressively presented parcels for a dinner party appetizer.

2 lemon grass stalks, very finely
   chopped
5ml/1 tsp galangal or fresh ginger,
   very finely chopped
4 garlic cloves, finely chopped
finely grated rind and juice of
   1 lime
4 spring onions (scallions),
   chopped
15ml/1 tbsp soy sauce
5ml/1 tsp Thai fish sauce
5ml/1 tsp chilli oil
45ml/3 tbsp chopped fresh
   coriander (cilantro)
30ml/2 tbsp chopped fresh Thai
   basil leaves
300g/10¼oz raw tiger prawns
   (shrimp), peeled and deveined
basil leaves and lime wedges, to
   garnish

Serves 4

NUTRITIONAL INFORMATION: Energy 105kcal/439kJ; Protein 16g; Carbohydrate 2g, of which sugars 1g; Fat 3g, of which saturates 0g; Cholesterol 0mg; Calcium 88mg; Fibre 0g; Sodium 463mg

1 Place the lemon grass, galangal, garlic, lime rind and juice and spring onions in a food processor. Blend in short bursts until the mixture forms a coarse paste.

2 Transfer the paste to a large bowl and stir in the soy sauce, fish sauce, chilli oil and chopped herbs.

3 Add the prawns to the paste and toss to coat evenly. Cover and marinate in the refrigerator for 30 minutes to 1 hour.

4 Cut out eight 20cm/8in squares of baking parchment. Place one-eighth of the prawn mixture in the centre of each one, then fold over the edges and twist closed to make a parcel.

5 Place the parcels in a large bamboo steamer, cover and steam over a wok of simmering water for 10 minutes, or until the prawns are just cooked through. Serve immediately, garnished with basil leaves and lime wedges.

Fasting tip When the prawns are peeled they should weigh about half as much. To make sure that your fasting day portion is the correct calorie total, your share of the prawns before cooking should be 75g/3oz.

SCALLOPS WITH FENNEL AND BACON

101 Calories

In this quick and easy recipe, low-calorie fennel is braised to provide a perfect base for luxurious scallops and a little salty bacon.

2 small fennel bulbs, trimmed and
    sliced, feathery tops reserved
8 large scallops, shelled
25g/1oz thinly sliced, lean smoked
    bacon or pancetta

Serves 2

NUTRITIONAL INFORMATION: Energy 101kcal/422kJ; Protein 17g; Carbohydrate 4g, of which sugars 3g; Fat 2g, of which saturates 1g; Cholesterol 28mg; Calcium 53mg; Fibre 3g; Sodium 347mg

1 Blanch the fennel slices in boiling water for about 3 minutes, until softened, then drain. Preheat the grill (broiler) to medium. Place the fennel in a shallow flameproof dish and season with salt and pepper. Grill (broil) for about 2–3 minutes, until the fennel is lightly browned.

2 Meanwhile, pat the scallops dry on kitchen paper and season lightly. Cook the bacon in a large, heavy frying pan, until crisp and golden. Drain and keep warm. Fry the scallops in the bacon fat for 1–2 minutes on each side, until cooked through.

3 Transfer the fennel to serving plates and crumble or snip the bacon into bite-size pieces over the top. Pile the scallops on the bacon and sprinkle with any reserved fennel tops.

PAN-STEAMED MUSSELS WITH THAI HERBS

66 Calories

Like so many Thai dishes, this is very easy to prepare, and is also very low in calories. The lemon grass and kaffir lime leaves add a refreshing tang to the mussels.

1kg/2¼lb fresh mussels, cleaned
    and scrubbed
2 lemon grass stalks, finely
    chopped
4 shallots, chopped
4 kaffir lime leaves, coarsely torn
2 fresh red chillies, sliced
15ml/1 tbsp Thai fish sauce
30ml/2 tbsp lime juice
thinly sliced spring onions
    (scallions) and coriander
    (cilantro) leaves, to serve

Serves 4

NUTRITIONAL INFORMATION: Energy 66kcal/276kJ; Protein 13g; Carbohydrate 4g, of which sugars 1g; Fat 2g, of which saturates Trace; Cholesterol 32mg; Calcium 40mg; Fibre 1g; Sodium 388mg

1 Discard any mussels that are broken or which do not close when tapped sharply. Place the mussels in a large, heavy pan and add the lemon grass, shallots, kaffir lime leaves, chillies, fish sauce and lime juice. Mix well. Cover the pan tightly and steam the mussels over a high heat, shaking the pan occasionally, for 5–7 minutes, until the shells have opened.

2 Transfer the mussels to individual bowls, discarding any mussels that have failed to open. Garnish with the sliced spring onions and coriander leaves. Serve immediately.

SKATE WINGS WITH ORANGE

216 Calories

Often served with black butter, skate is here teamed with sweet oranges and bitter salad leaves for a delicious taste contrast. Serve with toast for non-fasting diners.

800g/1¾lb skate wings
15ml/1 tbsp white wine vinegar
4 black peppercorns
fresh thyme sprig
15ml/1 tbsp white wine vinegar
15ml/1 tbsp olive oil
2 shallots, finely chopped
175g/6oz bitter salad leaves, such
   as frisée, radicchio and escarole
1 orange, peeled, membrane
   removed and sliced
2 medium tomatoes, peeled,
   seeded and diced
salt and ground black pepper

Serves 4

NUTRITIONAL INFORMATION: Energy 216kcal/903kJ; Protein 36g; Carbohydrate 2g, of which sugars 2g; Fat 7g, of which saturates 1g; Cholesterol 8mg; Calcium 111mg; Fibre 1g; Sodium 276mg

1 Put the skate wings into a large shallow pan, cover with cold water and add the vinegar, peppercorns and thyme. Bring to the boil, then reduce the heat and poach the fish gently for 8–10 minutes, until the flesh comes away easily from the bones.

2 Whisk the vinegar, olive oil and shallots together in a bowl. Season to taste. Tip the salad leaves into a bowl, pour over the dressing and toss well.

3 Flake the skate flesh from the bones, using a fork, and mix it into the salad. Add the orange slices and diced tomatoes, toss gently and serve.

CEVICHE WITH TOMATO SALSA

115 Calories

You can use almost any firm-fleshed fish for this South American dish, provided that it is perfectly fresh. Keep leftovers in the refrigerator for serving the next day.

225g/8oz fresh sea bass fillets, skinned and cut into strips
juice of 1½ limes
1 red chilli, finely chopped
salt

For the salsa
75g/2oz peeled avocado
2 medium firm tomatoes, peeled, seeded and diced
15ml/1 tbsp lemon juice
7.5ml/1½ tsp olive oil
15ml/1 tbsp fresh coriander (cilantro) leaves

Serves 4

NUTRITIONAL INFORMATION: Energy 115kcal/481kJ; Protein 12g; Carbohydrate 2g, of which sugars 2g; Fat 7g, of which saturates 1g; Cholesterol 45mg; Calcium 83mg; Fibre 1g; Sodium 45mg

1 Lay the fish in a shallow dish and pour over the lime juice, turning the strips to coat them all over in the juice. Cover with clear film (plastic wrap) and leave for 1 hour.

2 Season the fish with salt and sprinkle over the chillies. Toss the fish, then re-cover. Leave to marinate in the refrigerator for 15–30 minutes more.

3 For the salsa, cut the avocado into small dice and combine in a large bowl with the tomatoes, lemon juice and olive oil. Divide the salsa among four plates. Spoon on the ceviche, sprinkle with coriander and serve.

HERB AND CHILLI FISH CUSTARDS

211 Calories

Amino-acid rich eggs and fish are both great fasting day ingredients, complementing each other well to make a sustaining meal.

2 eggs
200ml/7fl oz/scant 1 cup light
   coconut milk
60ml/4 tbsp chopped coriander
   (cilantro)
1 red chilli, seeded and sliced
15ml/1 tbsp chopped lemon grass
2 kaffir lime leaves, finely shredded
30ml/2 tbsp red Thai curry paste
1 garlic clove, crushed
5ml/1 tsp finely grated ginger
2 spring onions (scallions), sliced
300g/11oz firm white fish fillets
   (cod or haddock), skinned
115g/4oz shelled prawns (shrimp)
salt and ground black pepper

Serves 4

NUTRITIONAL INFORMATION: Energy 211kcal/882kJ; Protein 25g; Carbohydrate 3g, of which sugars 2g; Fat 11g, of which saturates 1g; Cholesterol 162mg; Calcium 748mg; Fibre 1g; Sodium 266mg

1 Beat the eggs in a bowl, then stir in the coconut cream, coriander, chilli, lemon grass, lime leaves, curry paste, garlic, ginger and spring onions. Finely chop the fish and roughly chop the prawns and add to the egg mixture. Stir well and season.

2 Grease 4 ramekins with a little olive oil. Divide the fish mixture between them. In a steamer pan, bring plenty of water to the boil. Place the ramekins in the steamer.

3 Cover, reduce the heat to low and steam for 25–30 minutes, until set. Serve while hot. You could also steam these custards in a bain marie in the oven.

MARINATED SMOKED HADDOCK FILLETS

162 Calories

This tangy fish can be prepared in advance, as the flavours will just improve, so its ideal if you are coming home after a lean fasting day, and need supper quickly.

450g/1lb undyed smoked haddock
   fillet, skinned
1 onion, very thinly sliced
5ml/1 tsp Dijon mustard
10ml/2 tsp lemon juice
30ml/2 tbsp olive oil
15ml/1 tbsp chopped fresh dill
ground black pepper

Serves 4

NUTRITIONAL INFORMATION: Energy 162kcal/677kJ; Protein 22g; Carbohydrate 3g, of which sugars 2g; Fat 7g, of which saturates 1g; Cholesterol 41mg; Calcium 40mg; Fibre 1g; Sodium 98mg

1 Cut the fish fillet in half lengthways. Arrange in a single layer in a shallow dish. Sprinkle the onion rings evenly over the top.

2 Whisk together the mustard, lemon juice and some pepper. Gradually add the oil, whisking constantly, then stir in the dill.

3 Pour the dressing over the fish, cover with plastic wrap and leave for 2 hours in a cool place. To serve, slice thinly, top with onion rings and a little dressing, and serve with a green salad.

FILO-WRAPPED FISH

266 Calories

Pastry isn't usually part of a low-calorie diet, but filo is much lighter than shortcrust or puff pastry, and it creates a sealed package that means the fish keeps moist and tender. You could use cod in this recipe, which is lower in calories; the same amount of cod would reduce the calorie content to 172.

4 salmon steaks or fillets, total
   weight 350g/12oz
lemon juice
15ml/1 tbsp olive oil, plus extra for
   brushing
1 onion, chopped
2 celery sticks, chopped
1 green (bell) pepper, diced
2 garlic cloves, chopped
400g/14oz fresh or canned
   tomatoes, chopped
120ml/4fl oz/½ cup passata
   (bottled strained tomatoes)
30ml/2 tbsp chopped fresh flat leaf
   parsley
2–3 pinches of ground allspice or
   ground cloves
cayenne pepper, to taste
about 75g/2oz filo pastry (4 large
   sheets)
salt and ground black pepper

Serves 4

NUTRITIONAL INFORMATION: Energy 266kcal/1119kJ; Protein 22g; Carbohydrate 22g, of which sugars 8g; Fat 10g, of which saturates 2g; Cholesterol 44mg; Calcium 63mg; Fibre 2g; Sodium 205mg

1 Sprinkle the salmon or cod steaks or fillets with salt and black pepper and a squeeze of lemon juice. Set aside while you prepare the sauce.

2 Heat the olive oil in a pan, add the chopped onion, celery and pepper and fry for about 5 minutes, until the vegetables are softened. Add the garlic and cook for a further 1 minute, then add the tomatoes and passata and cook until the tomatoes are a thickened consistency.

3 Stir the parsley into the sauce, then season with allspice or cloves, cayenne pepper and salt and pepper. Preheat the oven to 200°C/400°F/Gas 6.

4 Take a sheet of filo pastry, brush with a little olive oil and fold in half. Place a piece of fish on top of the pastry, towards the bottom edge, then top with 1–2 spoonfuls of the sauce, spreading it evenly.

5 Roll the fish in the pastry, taking care to enclose the filling completely. Arrange on a baking sheet and repeat with the remaining pieces of fish and sheets of pastry. You should have about half the sauce remaining, to serve with the fish.

6 Bake the parcels for 10–15 minutes, until the pastry is golden. Meanwhile, reheat the remaining sauce if necessary. Serve the parcels immediately with the sauce.

PAPER-WRAPPED RED SNAPPER

128 Calories

This wrapped parcel effectively steams the fish inside, resulting in a beautifully fragrant and succulent meal. Serve with a little more asparagus on the side, and a fresh green salad, as the dish is very low in calories.

4 small, skinned red snapper fillets,
    each weighing 115g/4oz
8 asparagus spears, hard ends
    discarded
4 spring onions (scallions)
60ml/4 tbsp sake
grated rind of ½ lime
½ lime, thinly sliced and 5ml/1 tsp
    soy sauce, to serve
salt

Serves 4

Variation If you don't have any sake, use the same quantity of dry vermouth, or a little splash of lime or lemon juice instead.

NUTRITIONAL INFORMATION: Energy 128kcal/535kJ; Protein 24g; Carbohydrate 2g, of which sugars 1g; Fat 2g, of which saturates Trace; Cholesterol 42mg; Calcium 65mg; Fibre 1g; Sodium 205mg

1 Sprinkle the red snapper fillets with salt on both sides and set aside. Preheat the oven to 180°C/350°F/Gas 4.

2 Cut 2.5cm/1in from the tip of the asparagus, and slice in half lengthways. Slice the asparagus stems and spring onions diagonally into thin ovals. Par-boil the tips for 1 minute in lightly salted water and drain. Set aside.

3 Lay four pieces of baking parchment, each measuring 38x30cm/15x12in, on a work surface. Divide the asparagus slices and the spring onions between them. Sprinkle with salt and place a piece of fish on top. Add more salt and some sake, then sprinkle on the lime rind.

4 Lift the paper up, fold over the pieces, towards the contents, fold the ends into triangles and then tuck them underneath to make four airtight parcels.

5 Pour hot water from a kettle into a deep roasting pan fitted with a wire rack to 1cm/½in below the rack. Place the parcels on the rack. Cook in the centre of the preheated oven for 20 minutes. Check to see if it's cooked by carefully unfolding a parcel from one triangular side. The fish should have changed from translucent to white.

6 Transfer the parcels on to individual plates. Unfold the ends and lift open the middle a little. Insert a thin slice of lime and place two asparagus tips on top. Serve immediately, adding a little dash of soy sauce.

BAKED SEA BASS WITH FENNEL

212 Calories

Sea bass is a robust fish that makes a satisfying meal when teamed with peppers and fennel. For the correct portion you should have 85g/3oz of cooked fish.

4 fennel bulbs, trimmed and
    quartered lengthways
4 tomatoes, peeled and diced
8 anchovy fillets, cut in strips
a large pinch of saffron threads,
    soaked in 30ml/2 tbsp hot water
150ml/¼ pint/⅔ cup chicken or
    fish stock
2 red or yellow (bell) peppers,
    seeded and cut into strips
4 garlic cloves, chopped
15ml/1 tbsp chopped fresh
    marjoram
30ml/2 tbsp olive oil
1 whole sea bass, weighing about
    1.75kg/4lb, scaled and cleaned
salt and ground black pepper

Serves 4

NUTRITIONAL INFORMATION: Energy 212kcal/886kJ; Protein 21g; Carbohydrate 1g, of which sugars 10g; Fat 10g, of which saturates 2g; Cholesterol 4mg; Calcium 77mg; Fibre 5g; Sodium 587mg

1 Preheat the oven to 200°C/400°F/Gas 6. Cook the fennel in lightly salted boiling water for 5 minutes. Drain and arrange in a shallow ovenproof dish. Season with pepper.

2 Spoon the diced tomatoes and anchovy strips on top of the fennel. Stir the saffron and its soaking water into the stock and pour the mixture over the tomatoes. Lay the strips of pepper alongside the fennel and sprinkle with the garlic and marjoram. Drizzle 15ml/1 tbsp of the olive oil over the peppers and season with salt and pepper.

3 Bake the vegetables for 15 minutes. Season the sea bass inside and out and lay it on top of the fennel and pepper mixture. Drizzle the remaining olive oil over the fish and bake for 30–40 minutes more, until the sea bass is tender. To serve, remove the skin, and lift the fish away from the bone.

ROAST COD WRAPPED IN PROSCIUTTO

187 Calories

Wrapping chunky fillets of cod in wafer-thin slices of prosciutto keeps the fish succulent and moist, at the same time adding flavour and visual impact.

2 thick, skinless cod fillets, each
   weighing about 375g/13oz
75g/3oz thinly sliced prosciutto
400g/14oz cherry tomatoes, on the
   vine if possible
30ml/2 tbsp extra virgin olive oil
salt and ground black pepper

Serves 4

NUTRITIONAL INFORMATION: Energy 187kcal/784kJ; Protein 23g; Carbohydrate 3g, of which sugars 3g; Fat 9g, of which saturates 2g; Cholesterol 43mg; Calcium 15mg; Fibre 1g; Sodium 439mg

1 Preheat the oven to 220°C/425°F/Gas 7. Pat the fish dry on kitchen paper and remove any stray bones. Season lightly on both sides with salt and pepper.

2 Lay the prosciutto in a single layer in an ovenproof dish and place one cod fillet on top and at one end. Cover with the second fillet, laying the thick end on top of the thin end. Roll the fish in the prosciutto slices, tucking in the ends.

3 Place the tomatoes, still on their stalk, on each side of the rolled fish. Drizzle the tomatoes and prosciutto with the oil and season with black pepper. Roast for 35 minutes. Slice thickly and serve with the tomatoes, drizzled with the cooking juices.

GRILLED HAKE WITH LEMON AND CHILLI

188 Calories

This low-fat recipe is ideal for fasting days. The fish is cooked with the skin, which shouldn't be eaten. Serve with 55g/2oz green beans, which will add 12 calories.

4 hake fillets, 150g/5oz each
30ml/2 tbsp olive oil
1 lemon, rind grated and juice
    squeezed
15ml/1 tbsp crushed chilli flakes
salt and ground black pepper

Serves 4

NUTRITIONAL INFORMATION: Energy 188kcal/786kJ; Protein 27g; Carbohydrate 0g, of which sugars 0g; Fat 9g, of which saturates 1g; Cholesterol 35mg; Calcium 22mg; Fibre 0g; Sodium 150mg

1 Preheat the grill (broiler) to high. Brush the hake fillets all over with the olive oil and place them skin side up on a baking sheet.

2 Grill (broil) the fish for 4–5 minutes, until the skin is golden, then carefully turn them over using a metal spatula. Sprinkle the fillets with the lemon rind and chilli flakes and season with salt and ground black pepper.

3 Grill the fillets for a further 2–3 minutes, or until the hake is cooked through. (Test using the point of a sharp knife; the flesh should flake.) Squeeze over the lemon juice and serve.

COD WITH CHICKPEAS

193 Calories

This is made with salt cod, which needs to be soaked overnight in several changes of water before it can be cooked. Serve with a spinach salad, if you wish.

1 medium tomato
250g/9oz salt cod, soaked for
    24 hours in several changes
    of water
250g/8oz canned chickpeas, rinsed
1 small onion, chopped
1 small bunch of coriander
    (cilantro), chopped
15ml/2 tbsp olive oil
15ml/2 tbsp white wine vinegar
black pepper

Serves 4

NUTRITIONAL INFORMATION: Energy 193kcal/807kJ; Protein 17g; Carbohydrate 12g, of which sugars 2g; Fat 9g, of which saturates 1g; Cholesterol 29mg; Calcium 90mg; Fibre 3g; Sodium 218mg

1 Cut the tomato into quarters, scoop out the seeds and dice the flesh. Place the cod in boiling water and let it stand, away from the heat, for 5 minutes. Then drain the water and slice the fish (cleaned of skin and bones).

2 Put the cod, chickpeas, onion and coriander in a serving dish and mix gently. Add olive oil and vinegar to taste and toss lightly. Sprinkle with the diced tomato and serve.

Fasting tip Leftovers can be stored in the refrigerator and used for lunch the next day.

COD AND BEAN STEW WITH SAFFRON

215 Calories

A great warming winter dish, this has hearty Spanish flavours and for a low-calorie dish is beautifully filling. Serve with a pile of green leaves dressed with lemon.

15ml/1 tbsp olive oil
2 garlic cloves, finely chopped
1 onion, sliced
10ml/2 tsp paprika
5ml/1 tsp smoked Spanish paprika
large pinch of saffron threads,
    soaked in 45ml/3 tbsp hot water
1 x 400g/14oz can butter (lima)
    beans, rinsed
600ml/1 pint/2½ cups fish stock
1 red (bell) pepper, seeded and cut
    into chunks
6 plum tomatoes, quartered
350g/12oz skinned cod fillet, cut
    into large chunks
a handful fresh coriander (cilantro)
salt and ground black pepper

Serves 4

NUTRITIONAL INFORMATION: Energy 215kcal/899kJ; Protein 23g; Carbohydrate 20g, of which sugars 9g; Fat 5g, of which saturates 1g; Cholesterol 40mg; Calcium 50mg; Fibre 5g; Sodium 675mg

1 Heat the oil in a pan, add the garlic, fry for 2 minutes, then add the onion. Cover, and cook for about 5 minutes until the onion is soft. Stir in the paprikas, the saffron with its water, and salt and pepper.

2 Stir the beans into the pan and add just enough stock to cover. Bring to the boil and simmer, uncovered, for about 15 minutes, stirring occasionally to prevent sticking. Stir in the chopped pepper and tomato quarters.

3 Drop in the chunks of cod and bury them in the sauce. Cover and simmer for 5 minutes until cooked. Roughly chop the coriander, stir into the stew, and serve.

CHICKEN WITH WALNUT SAUCE

 **227** Calories

This Russian recipe is considerably less indulgent than it might initially appear. The creamy walnut sauce coats the succulent chicken making a satisfying and sustaining meal. Served with a couple of new small potatoes, it would still come in at less than 300 calories. Any leftovers can be refrigerated for the next day.

4 chicken breast fillets, total
   weight 500g/1¼lb, skin
   removed
500ml/17fl oz/generous 2 cups
   water
5ml/1 tsp salt
30ml/2 tbsp rapeseed (canola) oil
2 onions, chopped
2 garlic cloves, finely chopped
55g/2oz/1 cup walnut halves
5ml/1 tsp ground coriander
pinch of cayenne pepper
fresh coriander (cilantro), to
   garnish

Serves 6

NUTRITIONAL INFORMATION: Energy 227kcal/949kJ; Protein 20g; Carbohydrate 5g, of which sugars 3g; Fat 15g, of which saturates 2g; Cholesterol 71mg; Calcium 36mg; Fibre 1g; Sodium 398mg

1 Put the chicken in a medium pan and pour over enough cold water to cover. Bring to the boil, reduce the heat and simmer for 5 minutes, skimming the surface if necessary. Add the salt, cover and cook for a further 15 minutes.

2 Heat the oil in a small frying pan. Add the chopped onions and garlic and fry for 5 minutes, until softened but not browned. Add a splash of water if they begin to stick.

3 Transfer the onion and garlic to a food processor. Add the walnuts, coriander and cayenne pepper and half of the stock from the chicken. Process until a smooth paste is formed. Add more stock, a little at a time, until you have a sauce-like consistency. Transfer to a large bowl.

4 Cut the cooked chicken into 3cm/1¼in chunks. Add to the sauce and stir until the chicken is coated in the sauce. Cover and chill overnight.

5 To serve, turn the chicken into a serving dish. Garnish with walnut halves, if you wish, and coriander leaves.

Fasting tips
• Add a few walnut halves as a garnish if you have some calories to spare; three halves is 69kcals.
• Use any remaining chicken stock in a soup, or freeze for using another time.
• Serve larger portions, accompanied with buttered new potatoes and green beans, to non-fasting family members.

YELLOW CHICKEN CURRY

159 Calories

Using light coconut milk for this recipe gives a lower calorie count. Serve with 50g/2oz cooked egg noodles, which will add on 69 calories, if you wish.

1 fresh red chilli, thinly sliced
4 garlic cloves, coarsely chopped
3 shallots, coarsely chopped
2 lemon grass stalks, sliced
5ml/1 tsp ground turmeric
2.5ml/½ tsp shrimp paste
2.5ml/½ tsp salt
300ml/½ pint/1¼ cups chicken stock
30ml/2 tbsp thick tamarind juice
200ml/7fl oz/scant 1 cup light coconut milk
1 green papaya, peeled, seeded and thinly sliced
250g/9oz skinless, boneless chicken breast portions, diced
2 limes, 1 squeezed

Serves 4

NUTRITIONAL INFORMATION: Energy 159kcal/665kJ; Protein 15g; Carbohydrate 8g, of which sugars 4g; Fat 8g, of which saturates 1g; Cholesterol 53mg; Calcium 32mg; Fibre 1g; Sodium 793mg

1 Make the yellow curry paste. Put the red chilli, garlic, shallots, lemon grass and turmeric in a mortar or food processor. Add the shrimp paste and salt. Pound or process to a paste, adding a little water if necessary.

2 Pour the stock into a wok or medium pan and bring it to the boil. Stir in the curry paste. Bring back to the boil and add the tamarind juice and coconut milk.

3 Add the papaya and chicken and cook over a medium to high heat for about 15 minutes, stirring frequently, until the chicken is cooked. Stir in the juice of 1 lime.

4 Transfer to a warm dish and serve immediately, garnished with lime halves for squeezing.

TURKEY STEAKS WITH LIME

192 Calories

This is a lovely tangy dish that keeps well if you have any leftovers. Serve with tomatoes (85g/3oz adds 14 calories), and sautéed potatoes for non-fasting diners.

600g/1lb 6oz thin turkey steaks
10ml/2 tsp dried oregano
3 ripe limes, 2 juiced and 1 sliced into wedges
1 garlic clove
15ml/1 tbsp extra virgin olive oil
sea salt and ground black pepper

Serves 4

NUTRITIONAL INFORMATION: Energy 192kcal/803kJ; Protein 37g; Carbohydrate 4g, of which sugars 1g; Fat 2g, of which saturates 0g; Cholesterol 85mg; Calcium 46mg; Fibre 0g; Sodium 75mg

1 Place the turkey steaks between sheets of clear film (plastic wrap) and beat with a rolling pin until as thin as possible.

2 Spread them out in a shallow dish and sprinkle with the oregano. Drizzle with the lime juice and season with salt and pepper. Cover and leave to marinate at room temperature for about 1 hour.

3 Lift out the turkey slices and pat them dry with kitchen paper. Pour the olive oil into a frying pan. Add the garlic and when it sizzles, add as many of the turkey slices as the pan will hold in a single layer. Fry quickly, for only 1–2 minutes on each side, until cooked through. Keep hot while cooking the remaining slices.

4 Serve the turkey with the juices in the pan with lime wedges, accompanied by fresh tomatoes, if you wish.

SOY-MARINATED CHICKEN

167 Calories

This chicken dish is packed with flavour, and is delicious served on a bed of asparagus, or with shredded greens, for a complete low-calorie supper.

4 skinless, chicken breast fillets, total weight 450g/1lb
1 large orange
30ml/2 tbsp dark soy sauce

Serves 4

Fasting tip Serve leftovers the next day, wrapped with salad in a soft tortilla.

NUTRITIONAL INFORMATION: Energy 167kcal/698kJ; Protein 25g; Carbohydrate 5g, of which sugars 5g; Fat 5g, of which saturates 2g; Cholesterol 95mg; Calcium 35mg; Fibre 1g; Sodium 630mg

1 Slash each chicken portion and place in a shallow, ovenproof dish. Halve the orange. Squeeze one half over the chicken, with the soy sauce. Cover and leave to marinate for several hours.

2 Preheat the oven to 180°C/350°F/Gas 4. Cut the remaining orange half into wedges and place in the dish. Bake, uncovered, for 15–20 minutes until cooked through. Serve hot or cold.

VEAL-STUFFED CABBAGE LEAVES

271 Calories

This classic all-in-one dish has many variations. The filling in this version uses leaner veal, rather than pork, and makes a complete meal that can be prepared in advance.

1 Savoy cabbage, core removed, rinsed under cold running water, but left whole
300g/10½oz/1½ cups minced (ground) veal
small bunch parsley, chopped
115g/4oz/generous ½ cup long grain rice
1 small onion, finely chopped
50ml/2fl oz/¼ cup lemon juice
25ml/1½ tbsp water
salt and ground black pepper

Serves 4

NUTRITIONAL INFORMATION: Energy 271kcal/1133kJ; Protein 21g; Carbohydrate 33g, of which sugars 8g; Fat 7g, of which saturates 3g; Cholesterol 45mg; Calcium 118mg; Fibre 5g; Sodium 74mg

1 Put the whole cabbage in a large pan filled with hot water and simmer for 15–18 minutes, or until the leaves are soft. Drain and carefully remove the leaves. Preheat the oven to 160°C/325°F/Gas 3.

2 To make the filling, mix together the veal, parsley, rice and onion. Season well. Spread each cabbage leaf out and put a spoonful of the meat mixture in the centre. Fold over the top and roll up, tucking in both sides to make a small parcel.

3 Use wooden cocktail sticks (toothpicks) to secure the parcels during cooking. Put them in a single layer, seam side down, in a wide but deep dish. Add the lemon juice with 25ml/1½ tbsp water to the dish, then cover with foil. Cook in the oven for 1–1½ hours. Remove the cocktail sticks, and serve.

PORK AND VEAL RISSOLES

158 Calories

These juicy rissoles can be chargrilled or baked, and eaten with a tomato and onion salad. Non-fasting diners can eat the rissoles stuffed into griddled pitta breads.

350g/12oz/generous 1½ cups minced (ground) pork
200g/7oz/scant 1 cup minced (ground) veal
2 medium onions, grated
30ml/2 tbsp ground cumin
1.5ml/¼ tsp ground black pepper
salt

Serves 6

NUTRITIONAL INFORMATION: Energy 158kcal/660kJ; Protein 18g; Carbohydrate 3g, of which sugars 2g; Fat 8g, of which saturates 3g; Cholesterol 59mg; Calcium 18mg; Fibre 1g; Sodium 196mg

1 Put the pork and veal in a large bowl with the onion, cumin, pepper and salt, and combine. Cover and chill in the refrigerator for 2 hours.

2 When ready to cook the rissoles, preheat the grill (broiler) or a barbecue to a hot temperature. Add 120ml/4fl oz/½ cup water to the meat mixture and mix to combine.

3 Divide the meat into 12, and shape into long sausage shapes. Grill (broil) for 5 minutes on each side, or until the juices run clear. Serve them hot, or at room temperature, with a salad, if you like.

THAI BEEF STEW

More of a soup than a stew, this is a light and very easy to make main course meal. Serve with zero-calorie rice, or 50g/2oz cooked egg noodles (69 calories).

1 litre/1¾ pints/4 cups vegetable
  or chicken stock
450g/1lb lean beef steak, cut into
  slivers
3 garlic cloves, finely chopped
2 cinnamon sticks
4 star anise
30ml/2 tbsp light soy sauce
30ml/2 tbsp Thai fish sauce
2.5ml/½ tsp sugar
115g/4oz/1⅓ cups beansprouts
1 spring onion (scallion), finely
  chopped
small bunch of fresh coriander
  (cilantro), chopped

Serves 4

NUTRITIONAL INFORMATION: Energy 184kcal/769kJ; Protein 25g; Carbohydrate 4g, of which sugars 2g; Fat 7g, of which saturates 3g; Cholesterol 68mg; Calcium 15mg; Fibre 0g; Sodium 1106mg

1 Pour the stock into a large heavy pan. Add the beef, garlic, cinnamon sticks, star anise, soy sauce, fish sauce and sugar. Bring to the boil, then reduce the heat to low and simmer for 30 minutes. Skim off any foam that rises to the surface of the liquid with a slotted spoon.

2 Meanwhile, divide the beansprouts among four individual serving bowls. Remove and discard the cinnamon sticks and star anise from the stew with a slotted spoon.

3 Ladle the stew over the beansprouts, garnish with the chopped spring onion and chopped fresh coriander, and serve.

BEEF CURRY WITH AUBERGINES

192 Calories

This recipe needs good quality beef; sirloin is probably the best cut, as it is tender and full of flavour. Make sure the cut is lean, so you don't add in extra calories.

15ml/1 tbsp vegetable oil
20ml/4 tsp Thai green curry paste
200ml/7fl oz/scant 1 cup light
    coconut milk
300g/10½oz sirloin steak, fat
    trimmed off, cut into strips
2 kaffir lime leaves, torn
10ml/2 tsp Thai fish sauce
75g/3oz aubergine (eggplant), cut
    into bite-sized cubes
a small handful of fresh basil

Serves 4

NUTRITIONAL INFORMATION: Energy 192kcal/803kJ; Protein 19g; Carbohydrate 3g, of which sugars 2g; Fat 12g, of which saturates 2g; Cholesterol 38mg; Calcium 14mg; Fibre 1g; Sodium 232mg

1 Heat the oil in a large frying pan. Add the curry paste and cook for 1–2 minutes, until it is fragrant. Stir in half the coconut milk, a little at a time. Cook, stirring frequently, for about 5–6 minutes, until an oily sheen appears on the surface of the liquid.

2 Add the beef to the pan with the kaffir lime leaves, Thai fish sauce, sugar and aubergine cubes. Cook for 2–3 minutes, then stir in the remaining coconut milk.

3 Bring back to a simmer and cook for 4–5 minutes until the aubergines are tender. Stir in the Thai basil just before serving.

SEARED BEEF AND MANGO

187 Calories

This is another great way to make the most of a small amount of high-quality beef, flavoured with salty soy sauce and teamed up with sweet mango.

200g/7oz sirloin steak, trimmed
7.5ml/1½ tsp olive oil
30ml/2 tbsp soy sauce
½ medium mango
ground black pepper

Serves 2

NUTRITIONAL INFORMATION: Energy 187kcal/782kJ; Protein 25g; Carbohydrate 22g, of which sugars 21g; Fat 8g, of which saturates 3g; Cholesterol 51mg; Calcium 25mg; Fibre 4g; Sodium 873mg

1 Put the steak in a shallow dish and add the oil and soy sauce. Season with pepper, cover and chill for 2 hours.

2 Peel, pit and finely slice the mango, and set aside. Heat a griddle pan until hot. Remove the steak from the soy sauce marinade and place on the griddle pan. Cook for 3–5 minutes on each side.

3 Transfer the steak to a board and rest for 5–10 minutes. Pour the marinade into the pan and sizzle for a few seconds. Thinly slice the steak, and arrange on plates with the mango. Drizzle over the pan juices and serve.

EGG DISHES

After some unjustified bad press, eggs have made a comeback as part of a healthy diet. The concern over possible negative effects they had on raising blood cholesterol levels have been disproved, and heart health guidelines have been revised.

There is now no recommended upper limit on egg consumption. A small egg contains around 80 calories and 6g fat, but also has 7g protein, and provides B vitamins, vitamin D, and minerals. Within a balanced diet, and even more so on a fasting day, eggs are a useful non-meat protein source and offer huge versatility in the kitchen for quick snacks or more elaborate baked dishes.

◀Chilli salad omelette wraps.
▼ Coddled eggs.

QUINOA AND SALMON FRITTATA

215 Calories

Of Italian origin, frittata is a versatile dish, made more substantial than an omelette with the addition of meat, fish and vegetables. Here South American quinoa, increasingly popular as a gluten-free source of protein, iron and calcium, contributes to a hearty one-dish supper for all the family.

15ml/1 tbsp olive oil
1 medium onion, finely diced
1 red or orange (bell) pepper, chopped
2 cloves garlic, crushed
5ml/1 tsp fennel seeds
75g/3oz watercress or rocket (arugula), roughly chopped
30ml/2 tbsp crème fraîche
6 eggs, beaten
a handful of parsley, finely chopped
100g/4oz smoked salmon, cut into thin strips
115g/4oz/ ⅔ cup cooked red quinoa
50g/2oz/ ½ cup grated Parmesan
salt and ground black pepper

Serves 6

NUTRITIONAL INFORMATION: Energy 215kcal/899kJ; Protein 16g; Carbohydrate 8g, of which sugars 4g; Fat 13g, of which saturates 5g; Cholesterol 214mg; Calcium 153mg; Fibre 1g; Sodium 453mg

1 Heat the oil in a heavy frying pan and add the onion and chopped pepper. Stir-fry for 8–10 minutes until the onion is soft, then add the garlic and fennel seeds. Cook for 2 minutes.

2 Add the watercress or rocket and cook for a few more minutes until the leaves have wilted.

3 Meanwhile, whisk the crème fraîche, parsley and seasoning into the beaten eggs.

4 Add the salmon and quinoa to the frying pan, mix well, then spread evenly over the base of the pan.

5 Pour the beaten egg mixture into the pan, lower the heat, and cook for 5–8 minutes until the frittata is cooked most of the way through (you can test this by carefully pressing it with a fork). Covering the pan with a lid will help ensure even cooking. Heat the grill (broiler) to medium.

6 Sprinkle the grated cheese over the top of the frittata, then place under the grill, making sure the handle is not exposed to heat, for 3–5 minutes until the frittata is puffed and golden brown. Serve in slices, warm or at room temperature.

Fasting tips
• Leftovers can be kept in the refrigerator or frozen in portions for your next fasting day.
• If eating with others, serve larger portions to non-fasting diners, accompanied by sautéed potatoes and a rocket and tomato salad.

FRITTATA WITH SUN-DRIED TOMATOES 231 Calories

Deliciously enlivened with tasty pieces of sun-dried tomato, this frittata would be a good portable lunch to take to the office, together with a handful of crudités.

6 sun-dried tomatoes, hydrated in hot water for 15 minutes
30ml/2 tbsp olive oil
1 small onion, finely chopped
pinch of fresh thyme
5 eggs
50g/2oz/²/₃ cup freshly grated Parmesan cheese
salt and ground black pepper
sprigs of thyme, to garnish

Serves 4

NUTRITIONAL INFORMATION: Energy 231kcal/966kJ; Protein 14g; Carbohydrate 5g, of which sugars 4g; Fat 17g, of which saturates 5g; Cholesterol 255mg; Calcium 190mg; Fibre 2g; Sodium 471mg

1 Pat dry the sun-dried tomatoes and cut into strips. Heat the oil in a large frying pan. Stir in the onion and cook for 5–6 minutes or until golden. Add the sun-dried tomatoes and thyme, and season with salt and ground black pepper.

2 Beat the eggs and a little water in a bowl, and stir in the Parmesan cheese. Increase the heat under the pan and when the oil is sizzling, pour in the egg mixture and mix in, then cook without stirring on a medium heat for 5–6 minutes until set. Finish the frittata under a hot grill (broiler) for a few minutes, until the top is golden and bubbling. Serve sliced, warm or cold.

TRUFFLE OMELETTE 207 Calories

Give yourself a luxurious treat, even though it's a fasting day, and add some thinly sliced truffle to your supper in this beautifully-scented egg feast.

3 eggs
5g/¹/₄oz sliced fresh black truffle
15ml/1 tbsp virgin olive oil
sea salt and ground black pepper
a squeeze of lemon juice, to serve

Serves 2

NUTRITIONAL INFORMATION: Energy 207kcal/865kJ; Protein 13g; Carbohydrate 2g, of which sugars 0g; Fat 17g, of which saturates 4g; Cholesterol 391mg; Calcium 60mg; Fibre 1g; Sodium 142mg

1 Beat the eggs together in a small bowl, then season them with salt and pepper. Mix the sliced truffles into the beaten egg.

2 Heat the oil in a large frying pan and swirl it around to coat it thoroughly. Pour the egg and truffle mixture into the frying pan. As it begins to set, pull the outer edge of the frittata towards the centre and tip the pan so the egg mixture fills the gap.

3 When golden brown and set, fold the omelette in half and transfer to a serving plate. Divide into two, and serve at once with a squeeze of lemon.

FRESH HERB FRITTATA

197 Calories

This frittata makes the most of the fresh summer herbs that grow in every Italian countryside garden; any soft-leaved herbs can be used.

30ml/2 tbsp virgin olive oil
1 garlic clove, chopped
5 small spring onions (scallions), chopped
small handful of fresh mint leaves, chopped
small handful of fresh lemon balm leaves, chopped
small handful of fresh flat leaf parsley leaves, chopped
small handful of fresh chervil leaves, chopped
6 eggs, lightly beaten
sea salt and ground black pepper

Serves 4

NUTRITIONAL INFORMATION: Energy 197kcal/823kJ; Protein 13g; Carbohydrate 16g, of which sugars 4g; Fat 1g, of which saturates Trace; Cholesterol 350mg; Calcium 76mg; Fibre 1g; Sodium 336mg

1 Put the oil in a non-stick frying pan and add 45ml/3 tbsp cold water. Add the garlic, spring onions and chopped herbs, and cook for 5 minutes, or until softened.

2 Season the beaten eggs with salt and pepper and pour into the frying pan, stir gently with a wooden spoon to combine, then cook without stirring until set and golden underneath.

3 Cover the frittata with a plate that is larger than the pan. Turn it over in one smooth movement, then slide the frittata back into the hot pan, and cook until the bottom is also golden. Serve warm or at room temperature, in slices.

SPICY TORTILLA

Traditional Spanish tortilla is packed with fried potato; this version uses parsnip, corn and peas instead, and is spiced up with fresh chillies.

30ml/2 tbsp vegetable oil
1 onion, finely chopped
2.5ml/½ tsp ground cumin
1 garlic clove, crushed
1 or 2 fresh green chillies, chopped
fresh coriander (cilantro) sprigs,
    chopped, plus extra, to garnish
1 firm tomato, chopped
1 small parsnip, cubed and boiled
25g/1oz/¼ cup cooked peas
25g/1oz/¼ cup corn
4 eggs, beaten
25g/1oz/¼ cup grated cheese
salt and ground black pepper

Serves 4

NUTRITIONAL INFORMATION: Energy 266kcal/1112kJ; Protein 11g; Carbohydrate 8g, of which sugars 4g; Fat 22g, of which saturates 5g; Cholesterol 241mg; Calcium 105mg; Fibre 2g; Sodium 144mg

1 Heat the vegetable oil in a frying pan, and fry the onion for a few minutes, then add the cumin, garlic, chillies, coriander, tomato, parsnip, peas and corn. Cook, stirring, until well blended. Season to taste with salt and ground black pepper.

2 Increase the heat and pour in the beaten eggs. Reduce the heat, cover and cook until the bottom layer is brown. Turn the tortilla over and sprinkle with the grated cheese. Place under a hot grill (broiler) and cook until the cheese has melted.

3 Garnish the tortilla with sprigs of coriander and serve in slices with a crisp green salad (30g/1oz leaves adds just 4 calories).

CHARD FRITTATA

This frittata has a huge amount of chard in it, a leafy green that is much valued for its nutritional value, which is high in vitamins A, K and C.

675g/1½lb chard leaves, washed
    and sliced into thin ribbons
5 eggs
30ml/2 tbsp olive oil
1 large onion, sliced
salt and ground black pepper

Serves 4

NUTRITIONAL INFORMATION: Energy 220kcal/920kJ; Protein 13g; Carbohydrate 10g, of which sugars 4g; Fat 15g, of which saturates 3g; Cholesterol 293mg; Calcium 145mg; Fibre 1g; Sodium 654mg

1 Steam the chard until wilted, then drain and press out any liquid with the back of a spoon. Beat the eggs in a large bowl and season well. Add the chard to the egg mixture.

2 Heat half the oil in a large frying pan. Add the onion and cook over a medium-low heat, covered, for about 10 minutes until soft, stirring often. Add the onions to the eggs and chard.

3 Heat the remaining oil in the frying pan over a medium-high heat. Pour in the egg mixture and reduce the heat to medium-low. Cook for 5–7 minutes until set. Finish the top of the frittata under a preheated grill (broiler) until golden. Serve warm, cut into wedges.

CHILLI SALAD OMELETTE WRAPS

These wafer-thin omelettes can be used instead of tortillas, for a low-calorie lunch. Here they are filled with a crisp salad and hummus. For picture, see page 110.

2 eggs
5ml/1 tsp cornflour (cornstarch)
    mixed with 10ml/2 tsp water
50g/2oz/½ cup shredded salad
    vegetables, such as crisp lettuce,
    carrot, celery, spring onion
    (scallions) and (bell) peppers
fresh red chilli, seeded and finely
    sliced, to taste
10ml/2 tsp olive oil
10ml/2 tsp white wine vinegar
30ml/2 tbsp hummus
salt and ground black pepper

Serves 2

NUTRITIONAL INFORMATION: Energy 168kcal/702kJ; Protein 9g; Carbohydrate 5g, of which sugars 1g; Fat 13g, of which saturates 3g; Cholesterol 234mg; Calcium 50mg; Fibre 1g; Sodium 578mg

1 Break an egg into a bowl. Add half the cornflour and water and beat well. Heat a lightly oiled frying pan and pour the egg mixture into the pan, tipping it to spread it out to a thin, even layer. Cook gently to avoid it colouring or becoming bubbly and crisp. Make a second omelette in the same way.

2 Toss the shredded vegetables and chilli in a bowl with the olive oil and vinegar, season well.

3 Spread half of each omelette with hummus, top with vegetables and fold in half, and serve.

STIR-FRY OMELETTE WRAPS

192 Calories

These pancake-like omelettes are made in the same way as the omelette wraps on the previous page, but this version is filled with a more substantial filling of stir-fried vegetables in black bean sauce. Serve these rolls with a generous portion of steamed green beans with garlic and a dash of soy sauce, for an evening meal.

50g/2oz broccoli, cut into small
   florets
15ml/1 tbsp groundnut (peanut) oil
small piece fresh root ginger,
   grated
½ large garlic clove, crushed
1 red chilli, seeded and finely
   sliced
2 spring onions (scallions), sliced
   diagonally
115g/4oz/1½ cups pak choi (bok
   choy), finely shredded
30ml/2 tbsp of fresh coriander
   (cilantro) leaves
50g/2oz/¼ cup beansprouts
30ml/2 tbsp black bean sauce
2 eggs
salt and freshly ground black
   pepper

Serves 2

NUTRITIONAL INFORMATION: Energy 192kcal/803kJ; Protein 12g; Carbohydrate 6g, of which sugars 4g; Fat 14g, of which saturates 3g; Cholesterol 234mg; Calcium 114mg; Fibre 2g; Sodium 855mg

1 Blanch the broccoli in boiling salted water for 2 minutes, drain, then refresh under cold running water.

2 Meanwhile, heat 15ml/1 tbsp of the oil in a frying pan or wok. Add the ginger, garlic and half of the chilli and stir-fry for 1 minute. Add the spring onions, broccoli and pak choi, and stir-fry for 2 minutes more, tossing the vegetables continuously to prevent sticking and to cook them evenly.

3 Chop three-quarters of the coriander and add to the frying pan or wok. Add the beansprouts and stir-fry for 1 minute, then add the black bean sauce and heat through for a further 1 minute. Remove the pan from the heat and keep warm.

4 Lightly mix one egg in a bowl with a fork and season well. Heat a little of the remaining oil in a small frying pan and add the beaten egg, swirling it around so that it covers the base of the pan completely. Then scatter over half of the reserved coriander leaves.

5 Cook on a low heat, to stop any bubbling or colouring, until set, then turn out the omelette on to a plate and keep warm. Make the second omelette in the same way.

6 To serve, spoon half of the vegetable stir-fry on to each of the omelettes and roll up. Cut in half crossways and serve.

BAKED HAM AND EGGS

This is a bit like a quiche Lorraine, but without the high-calorie pastry case. It makes a great family supper, or can be frozen in portions for future fast days.

30ml/2 tbsp vegetable oil, plus
   extra for greasing
1 leek, white and pale green parts
   only, thinly sliced, or 1 shallot,
   chopped
4 eggs
300ml/½ pint/1¼ cups skimmed
   milk
115g/4oz cooked lean ham,
   preferably smoked, diced
salt and ground black pepper

Serves 4

NUTRITIONAL INFORMATION: Energy 216kcal/903kJ; Protein 17g; Carbohydrate 5g, of which sugars 5g; Fat 15g, of which saturates 3g; Cholesterol 273mg; Calcium 142mg; Fibre 1g; Sodium 663mg

1 Preheat the oven to 180°C/350°F/Gas 4. Lightly oil an ovenproof dish measuring about 20cm/8in in diameter. Heat the oil in a pan, add the leek or shallot and fry for 2–3 minutes.

2 Break the eggs into a bowl and beat lightly together. Add the cream, season with salt and pepper and beat together until well combined. Add the chopped ham.

3 Pour the mixture into the prepared dish and bake in the oven for about 25 minutes, until set and golden brown. Serve hot.

CODDLED EGGS

These delicately-flavoured eggs, baked in the oven with a small amount of cream, have a lovely soft texture, and are ideal for a late supper.

butter, for greasing
2 large eggs
30ml/2 tbsp single (light) cream
salt and pepper
chopped fresh chives, to garnish

Serves 2

NUTRITIONAL INFORMATION: Energy 116kcal/485kJ; Protein 8g; Carbohydrate Trace, of which sugars 0g; Fat 9g, of which saturates 4g; Cholesterol 242mg; Calcium 48mg; Fibre 0g; Sodium 475mg

1 Butter two small ramekin dishes or cups and break an egg into each. Season, then top with a spoonful of cream. Cover with foil.

2 Put a wide, shallow pan over medium heat. Stand the covered dishes in the pan. Add boiling water to come half way up the sides of the dishes. Heat until the water just comes to the boil then cover and simmer gently for 1 minute.

3 Remove from the heat and leave to stand, still covered, for 10 minutes. Serve sprinkled with chives.

BAKED EGGS WITH LEEKS

This richer version of a baked egg recipe makes a satisfying dinner, served with some steamed asparagus or green beans. Spinach could be used instead of leeks.

5ml/1 tsp vegetable oil
115g/4oz leeks, thinly sliced
a few fresh sage leaves
30ml/2 tbsp thick cream
freshly grated nutmeg
2 eggs
salt and black pepper

Serves 2

NUTRITIONAL INFORMATION: Energy 171kcal/715kJ; Protein 9g; Carbohydrate 2g, of which sugars 2g; Fat 14g, of which saturates 6g; Cholesterol 245mg; Calcium 57mg; Fibre 1g; Sodium 468mg

1 Preheat the oven to 190°C/375°F/Gas 5. Lightly oil the base and sides of two ramekins.

2 Heat the oil in a pan and cook the leeks for 3–5 minutes over a medium heat, stirring. Add a few snipped sage leaves and stir in 15ml/1 tbsp of the cream. Cook over a gentle heat for 5 minutes. Season with salt, pepper and nutmeg.

3 Place the ramekins in a small roasting tin and divide the leeks between them. Break an egg into each, spoon over the remaining cream, and season. Pour boiling water into the tin to come about half way up the sides of the dishes. Bake for about 10 minutes, until just set. Top with a sage leaf and serve.

STIR-FRIES

A successful stir-fry depends on ingredients being prepared ahead, and cooked in a very hot wok in non-smoking oils. If you haven't got a wok, a heavy-based frying pan will be fine, but it needs to be big enough to toss the vegetables around. It is easy to mix and match the ingredients of a stir-fry, but make sure you measure them correctly to keep count of the total calories involved. All the recipes in this chapter serve two, but are pretty low in calories, so you might have enough allowance at the end of the day to eat both portions.

◀ Stir-fried Brussels sprouts.
▼ Stir-fried tofu and asparagus.

STIR-FRIED SQUID WITH GINGER

165 Calories

Usually a great way to pack in lots of vegetables, protein-based stir-fries can keep you satisfied for longer. When cooked quickly, squid can be beautifully tender.

4 ready-prepared baby squid, total
   weight 250g/9oz
15ml/1 tbsp vegetable oil
2 garlic cloves, finely chopped
30ml/2 tbsp soy sauce
2.5cm/1in piece fresh root ginger,
   peeled and finely chopped
juice of ½ lemon
5ml/1 tsp sugar
2 spring onions (scallions),
   chopped

Serves 2

NUTRITIONAL INFORMATION: Energy 165kcal/690kJ; Protein 20g; Carbohydrate 5g, of which sugars 4g; Fat 7g, of which saturates 1g; Cholesterol 27mg; Calcium 25mg; Fibre 0g; Sodium 1206mg

1 Rinse the squid well and pat dry with kitchen paper. Cut the bodies into rings and halve the tentacles, if necessary.

2 Heat the oil in a wok or frying pan and cook the garlic until golden brown, but do not let it burn. Add the squid and stir-fry for 30 seconds over a high heat.

3 Add the soy sauce, ginger, lemon juice, sugar and spring onions. Stir-fry for a further 30 seconds, then serve.

HOKI STIR-FRY

195 Calories

Any firm-fleshed white fish, such as monkfish or cod, can be used for this stir-fry. Vary the vegetables according to what is available.

225g/8oz hoki fillet, skinned and
   cut into strips
2.5ml/½ tsp five-spice powder
2 spring onions (scallions)
15ml/1 tbsp groundnut (peanut) oil
1cm/½in piece fresh root ginger,
   peeled and cut into thin slivers
1 garlic clove, finely chopped
100g/3½oz beansprouts
1 carrot, thinly sliced in batons
40g/1½oz mangetouts (snow
   peas), thinly sliced
40g/1½oz asparagus spears,
   trimmed and cut in half
4 baby corn
5ml/1 tsp soy sauce

Serves 2

NUTRITIONAL INFORMATION: Energy 195kcal/815kJ; Protein 23g; Carbohydrate 7g, of which sugars 5g; Fat 9g, of which saturates 2g; Cholesterol 0mg; Calcium 56mg; Fibre 2g; Sodium 297mg

1 Season the fish with salt, pepper and five-spice powder. Trim the spring onions and cut them diagonally into 2cm/¾in pieces, keeping the white and green parts separate. Set aside.

2 Heat a wok, then pour in the oil. As soon as it is hot, add the ginger and garlic. Stir-fry for 1 minute, then add the white parts of the spring onions and cook for 1 minute more.

3 Add the hoki strips and stir-fry for 2–3 minutes, until all the pieces of fish are opaque. Add the beansprouts. Toss them around to coat them in the oil, then put in the carrot batons, mangetout, asparagus and baby corn. Stir-fry for 3–4 minutes. Add the soy sauce, toss everything together, then stir in the green parts of the spring onions. Serve immediately.

STIR-FRIED PRAWNS

161 Calories

Tamarind gives a lovely sour, tangy flavour to this prawn dish. Serve with a big pile of steamed pak choi or other dark leafy greens. 115g/4oz pak choi adds 15 calories.

2 dried red chillies
15ml/1 tbsp vegetable oil
30ml/2 tbsp chopped onion
1 garlic clove, chopped
30ml/2 tbsp sliced shallots
5ml/1 tsp Thai fish sauce
30ml/2 tbsp tamarind juice
150g/5½oz raw prawns (shrimp),
   peeled
2 spring onions (scallions),
   chopped, to garnish

Serves 2

NUTRITIONAL INFORMATION: Energy 161kcal/673kJ; Protein 16g; Carbohydrate 7g, of which sugars 1g; Fat 7g, of which saturates 1g; Cholesterol 0mg; Calcium 73mg; Fibre 1g; Sodium 248mg

1 Heat a wok and add the dried chillies and dry-fry them for a few seconds. Set aside. Add the oil to the wok or pan, add the onion and cook over a medium heat, stirring, for 2–3 minutes.

2 Add the garlic and shallots, 30ml/2 tbsp water, fish sauce, dry-fried red chillies and tamarind juice, stirring. Bring to the boil, then lower the heat slightly.

3 Add the prawns. Toss over the heat for 3–4 minutes, until they are pink. Garnish with the spring onions and serve.

CASHEW CHICKEN STIR-FRY

287 Calories

This is a lovely tasty Thai recipe, which will satisfy your appetite. Cashew nuts are nutritious and filling, but high in calories – about 9 per nut – so measure carefully.

15ml/1 tbsp vegetable oil
1 garlic cloves, finely chopped
2 dried red chillies, crushed
175g/6oz boneless chicken breast
    fillets, skin removed and cut
    into bite-sized pieces
1 red (bell) pepper, diced
10ml/2 tsp oyster sauce
10ml/2 tsp soy sauce
pinch of sugar
4 spring onions (scallions), cut into
    5cm/2in lengths
28g/1oz/¼ cup cashews, roasted

Serves 2

NUTRITIONAL INFORMATION: Energy 287kcal/1200kJ; Protein 23g; Carbohydrate 10g, of which sugars 7g; Fat 17g, of which saturates 4g; Cholesterol 74mg; Calcium 28mg; Fibre 2g; Sodium 644mg

1 Preheat a wok and then heat the oil. Add the garlic and dried chillies to the wok and stir-fry over a medium heat until golden. Do not let the garlic burn, otherwise it will taste bitter.

2 Add the chicken to the wok and stir-fry until it is cooked through, then add the red pepper. If the mixture is very dry, add a little water.

3 Stir in the oyster sauce, soy sauce and sugar. Add the spring onions and cashew nuts. Stir-fry for 1–2 minutes more, until heated through. Spoon into a warm dish and serve.

DUCK STIR-FRY

263 Calories

Duck is a very rich meat, and you don't need very much to feel satisfied, especially when it is stir-fried with butternut squash in this delicious Chinese-style dish.

200g/7oz duck breast fillet, skinned and finely sliced
5ml/1 tsp five-spice powder
10ml/2 tsp sesame oil
grated rind and juice of ½ orange
5ml/1 tsp Thai red curry paste
10ml/2 tsp Thai fish sauce
150ml/¼ pint/¾ cup light coconut milk
115g/4oz peeled and cubed butternut squash, cooked
½ fresh red chilli, seeded and finely sliced
2 kaffir lime leaves, torn

Serves 2

NUTRITIONAL INFORMATION: Energy 263kcal/1099kJ; Protein 22g; Carbohydrate 10g, of which sugars 6g; Fat 17g, of which saturates 2g; Cholesterol 110mg; Calcium 125mg; Fibre 1g; Sodium 466mg

1 Place the duck in a bowl with the five-spice powder, sesame oil and orange rind and juice. Cover the bowl with clear film (plastic wrap) and marinate for at least 15 minutes.

2 Pour the marinade from the duck into a wok and heat until boiling. Stir in the curry paste and cook for 2–3 minutes. Add the duck and cook for 3–4 minutes, stirring, until browned.

3 Add the fish sauce and cook for 2 minutes more. Stir in the coconut milk, then add the cooked squash, with the chilli and lime leaves. Simmer gently, stirring frequently, for 5 minutes, then spoon into a dish, and serve.

STIR-FRIED TOFU AND ASPARAGUS

237 Calories

Tofu works well in stir-fries, absorbing the rich flavourings of Asian cooking. Here it is also adding non-meat protein for a balanced meal. For picture, see page 123.

200g/8oz firm tofu, cut in half
15ml/1 tbsp groundnut (peanut) oil
15ml/1 tbsp Thai green curry paste
30ml/2 tbsp soy sauce
2 kaffir lime leaves, rolled into cylinders and thinly sliced
5ml/1 tsp sugar
150ml/¼ pint/⅔ cup vegetable stock
250g/9oz asparagus, trimmed and sliced into 5cm/2in lengths
chopped fresh coriander (cilantro), to serve

Serves 2

NUTRITIONAL INFORMATION: Energy 237kcal/991kJ; Protein 17g; Carbohydrate 8g, of which sugars 6g; Fat 16g, of which saturates 3g; Cholesterol 0mg; Calcium 395mg; Fibre 2g; Sodium 1410mg

1 Preheat the grill (broiler) to medium and grill (broil) the tofu pieces for 2–3 minutes, then turn over and continue to cook until crisp and golden brown all over.

2 Heat the oil in a heavy frying pan. Add the green curry paste and cook over a medium heat, stirring, for 1–2 minutes. Stir the soy sauce, lime leaves, sugar and vegetable stock into the pan, bring to the boil, then reduce the heat to a simmer.

3 Add the asparagus and simmer gently for 5 minutes. Meanwhile, cut each piece of tofu into four, then add to the pan. Toss to coat, and serve in bowls, garnished with coriander.

STIR-FRIED BEEF IN OYSTER SAUCE

145 Calories

Mushrooms are a useful dieting food as they are very low in calories and contain a significant amount of water by weight. Most varieties are only around 15 calories per 115g/4oz, which is a very generous helping. They also contain useful fibre and micronutrients, and, of course, they taste delicious.

150g/5½oz lean rump (round)
    steak, trimmed
10ml/2 tsp soy sauce
5ml/1 tsp cornflour (cornstarch)
5ml/1 tsp vegetable oil
5ml/1 tsp chopped garlic
5ml/1 tsp chopped fresh root
    ginger
85g/3oz mixed mushrooms such as
    shiitake, oyster and straw
10ml/2 tsp oyster sauce
2.5ml/½ tsp sugar, optional
2 spring onions (scallions), cut into
    short lengths
ground black pepper
1 fresh red chilli, seeded and cut
    into strips, to garnish

Serves 2

NUTRITIONAL INFORMATION: Energy 145kcal/606kJ; Protein 19g; Carbohydrate 6g, of which sugars 1g; Fat 5g, of which saturates 2g; Cholesterol 44mg; Calcium 20mg; Fibre 1g; Sodium 1044mg

1 Place the steak in the freezer for 30–40 minutes, until firm, then, using a very sharp knife, slice it on the diagonal into long thin strips.

2 Mix together the soy sauce and cornflour in a large bowl. Add the steak to the bowl, turning to coat well. Cover with clear film (plastic wrap) and leave to marinate at room temperature for 1–2 hours.

3 Heat half the oil in a wok or large, heavy frying pan. Add the garlic and ginger and cook for 1–2 minutes, until fragrant.

4 Drain the steak, add it to the wok or pan and stir well to separate the strips. Cook, stirring frequently, for a further 1–2 minutes, until the steak is browned all over and tender. Remove from the wok or pan and set aside.

5 Heat the remaining oil in the wok or pan. Add the mushrooms and stir-fry over a medium heat until golden brown.

6 Return the steak to the wok and mix with the mushrooms. Spoon in the oyster sauce and sugar, if using, mix well, then add ground black pepper to taste. Toss over the heat until all the ingredients are thoroughly combined.

7 Stir in the spring onions. Tip the mixture on to a serving platter, garnish with the strips of red chilli and serve.

Fasting tip The sugar often added to stir-fries gives a characteristic sheen to the end result, but it can be left out if you wish. Without the sugar the calorie content would be reduced from 145kcal to 141kcal per portion.

STIR-FRIED PORK WITH DRIED SHRIMP 185 Calories

Dried shrimp is an intense paste available from Asian stores that adds a deep umami style flavour to this stir-fry. It is a great low-calorie flavouring.

115g/4oz lean pork fillet
   (tenderloin), sliced
15ml/1 tbsp vegetable oil
1 garlic clove, finely chopped
30ml/1 tbsp dried shrimp
2.5ml/½ tsp dried shrimp paste
15ml/1 tbsp soy sauce
juice of 1 lime
1 small fresh red or green chilli,
   seeded and finely chopped
4 pak choi (bok choy), shredded

Serves 2

NUTRITIONAL INFORMATION: Energy 185kcal/773kJ; Protein 23g; Carbohydrate 3g, of which sugars 3g; Fat 9g, of which saturates 2g; Cholesterol 112mg; Calcium 271mg; Fibre 2g; Sodium 1241mg

1 Place the pork in the freezer for about 30 minutes, until firm. Using a sharp knife, cut it into thin slices. Heat the oil in a wok and cook the garlic until golden brown.

2 Add the pork and stir-fry for about 4 minutes, until just cooked. Add the dried shrimp, then stir in the shrimp paste, with the soy sauce and lime juice. Add the chilli and pak choi and toss over the heat until the vegetables wilt.

3 Transfer the stir-fry to warm bowls and serve immediately.

STIR-FRIED SEEDS AND VEGETABLES

241 Calories

Full of slow-release seeds, and low-calorie vegetables, this stir-fry has a rich savoury sauce that is satisfying on fast days, and can be served with rice for non-fasters.

15ml/1 tbsp vegetable oil
15ml/1 tbsp each of sesame,
    sunflower and pumpkin seeds
1 garlic clove, finely chopped
2.5cm/1in fresh ginger, grated
1 large carrot, cut into batons
1 large courgette (zucchini), cut
    into batons
50g/2oz/1 cup oyster mushrooms,
    torn in pieces
115g/4oz spinach, chopped
small bunch of mint, chopped
30ml/2 tbsp black bean sauce
15ml/1 tbsp soy sauce
15ml/1 tbsp rice vinegar

Serves 2

NUTRITIONAL INFORMATION: Energy 241kcal/1007kJ; Protein 9g; Carbohydrate 9g, of which sugars 6g; Fat 19g, of which saturates 3g; Cholesterol 0mg; Calcium 196mg; Fibre 4g; Sodium 1003mg

1 Heat the oil in a wok or large frying pan. Add the seeds. Toss over a medium heat for 1 minute, then add the garlic and ginger and continue to stir-fry until the ginger is aromatic and the garlic is golden. Do not let the garlic burn.

2 Add the carrot and courgette batons and the torn mushrooms to the wok or pan and stir-fry over a medium heat for a further 5 minutes, or until all the vegetables are crisp-tender and golden at the edges.

3 Add the watercress or spinach with the fresh herbs. Toss over the heat for 1 minute, then stir in the black bean sauce, soy sauce, sugar and vinegar. Stir-fry for 1–2 minutes, until combined and hot. Serve immediately.

STIR-FRIED BRUSSELS SPROUTS

122 Calories

This is a great way of cooking sprouts, helping to retain their sweet flavour and crunchy texture. The bacon does raise the calorie count but adds protein and taste.

200g/7oz Brussels sprouts
15ml/1 tbsp sunflower oil
1 smoked lean (Canadian) bacon
   rasher (strip), chopped
5ml/1 tsp caraway seeds
salt and ground black pepper

Serves 2

NUTRITIONAL INFORMATION: Energy 122kcal/510kJ; Protein 8g; Carbohydrate 4g, of which sugars 3g; Fat 9g, of which saturates 2g; Cholesterol 6mg; Calcium 50mg; Fibre 4g; Sodium 273mg

1 Wash and trim the Brussels sprouts then cut them into fine shreds and set aside. Heat the oil in a wok or large frying pan and add the bacon. Cook for 1–2 minutes, or until the bacon is beginning to turn golden.

2 Add the shredded sprouts to the wok or pan and stir-fry for 1–2 minutes, or until lightly cooked.

3 Season the sprouts with salt and ground black pepper to taste and stir in the caraway seeds. Cook for a further 30 seconds, then serve immediately.

STIR-FRIED BROCCOLI WITH SESAME SEEDS

141 Calories

Purple sprouting broccoli has been used for this recipe, but when it is not available an ordinary variety of broccoli, such as calabrese, will also work very well.

225g/8oz purple sprouting broccoli
15ml/1 tbsp olive oil
15ml/1 tbsp soy sauce
15ml/1 tbsp sesame seeds
ground black pepper

Serves 2

NUTRITIONAL INFORMATION: Energy 141kcal/589kJ; Protein 6g; Carbohydrate 4g, of which sugars 3g; Fat 12g, of which saturates 2g; Cholesterol 0mg; Calcium 278mg; Fibre 5g; Sodium 930mg

1 Wash the broccoli and trim the ends. Heat the olive oil in a wok or large frying pan and add the broccoli. Stir-fry for 3–4 minutes, or until tender, adding a splash of water if the pan becomes too dry.

2 Meanwhile, in a small frying pan, lightly toast the sesame seeds until just golden.

3 Add the soy sauce to the broccoli, then season with ground black pepper to taste. Add the sesame seeds, toss to combine and serve immediately.

STIR-FRIED CARROTS WITH MANGO

217 Calories

This low-calorie dish can be served topped with a spoonful of natural yogurt and a green salad; 15ml/1 tbsp natural yogurt would add 15 calories.

5ml/1 tsp olive oil
½ onion, chopped
2.5cm/1in fresh ginger, grated
2 garlic cloves, chopped
3 carrots, sliced
15ml/1 tbsp shelled pistachio nuts,
  roasted
2.5ml/½ tsp ground cinnamon
5ml/1 tsp ras el hanout
250g/9oz peeled and coarsely
  diced ripe mango
small bunch of fresh coriander
  (cilantro), finely chopped
juice of ½ lemon
salt

Serves 2

NUTRITIONAL INFORMATION: Energy 217kcal/907kJ; Protein 4g; Carbohydrate 28g, of which sugars 26g; Fat 11g, of which saturates 1g; Cholesterol 0mg; Calcium 92mg; Fibre 6g; Sodium 24mg

1 Heat the olive oil in a heavy frying pan or wok. Stir in the onion, ginger and garlic and fry for 1 minute.

2 Add the carrots to the pan, tossing them to make sure that they are thoroughly mixed with the flavouring ingredients, and cook until they begin to brown.

3 Add the pistachio nuts, cinnamon and ras el hanout to the pan, then gently mix in the diced mango.

4 Sprinkle with fresh coriander, season with salt and pour over the lemon juice. Serve immediately.

SALADS

It is probably not surprising that salads feature in a low-calorie cookbook, and here is an inspired collection using fresh ingredients, enhanced by flavourings from around the world. Avoiding oil-based dressings on fasting days doesn't mean you also have to skimp on delicious herbs, spices, chilli, soy sauce or a sprinkling of seeds to add taste and textures. These salads can accompany recipes from other chapters, or be eaten as a dish in their own right, particularly if they also include protein. Vary the ingredients depending on what is in season, but check with the food charts to keep track of any changes in total calorie counts.

◀ White cabbage slaw.
▼ Beetroot and orange salad.

ASPARAGUS AND LANGOUSTINE SALAD

278 Calories

Low-fat langoustines are often sold frozen and shelled. They vary in size, so make sure you don't use more than the recipe weight for an accurate calorie count.

8 asparagus spears, trimmed
1 carrot, cut into fine strips
10ml/2 tsp olive oil
1 garlic clove, peeled
about 8 cooked langoustines
    (Dublin Bay prawns), 175g/6oz
    total weight when shelled
15ml/1 tbsp fresh tarragon,
    chopped

For the dressing
15ml/1 tbsp tarragon vinegar
30ml/2 tbsp olive oil
salt and ground black pepper

Serves 2

NUTRITIONAL INFORMATION: Energy 278kcal/1162kJ; Protein 22g; Carbohydrate 5g, of which sugars 4g; Fat 18g, of which saturates 3g; Cholesterol 140mg; Calcium 108mg; Fibre 2g; Sodium 183mg

1 Cut the asparagus spears in half, steam lightly until tender, and place in a shallow dish. Blanch the carrot strips for two minutes, drain, refresh under cold running water, and add to the dish with the asparagus.

2 Make the dressing. Whisk the vinegar with the oil in a small bowl. Season to taste. Pour over the asparagus and carrot and leave to absorb the flavours.

3 Heat the oil with the garlic in a frying pan until very hot. Add the langoustines and sauté quickly until heated through.

4 Divide the asparagus and carrot on two plates, top each portion with four langoustines, drizzle over the dressing left in the dish and sprinkle the chopped tarragon on top.

SKATE SALAD WITH MUSTARD DRESSING 151 Calories

This is a fresh salad full of flavour. Once cooked, skate can be easily pulled from its cartilage-like bones. Calories per helping are based on 600g/1lb 3oz cooked fish.

750g/1lb 8oz skate wings
15ml/1 tbsp white wine vinegar
15 peppercorns
1 thyme sprig
115g/4oz rocket (arugula)
115g/4oz watercress
200g/7oz mixed salad leaves
2 tomatoes, seeded and diced
finely pared orange zest, to garnish

For the dressing
30ml/2 tbsp grated crisp pear
15ml/1 tbsp virgin olive oil
15ml/1 tbsp white wine vinegar
1 clove garlic, crushed
10ml/2 tsp English (hot) mustard
5ml/1 tsp soy sauce
salt and ground black pepper

Serves 4

NUTRITIONAL INFORMATION: Energy 151kcal/631.18kJ; Protein 24g; Carbohydrate 4g, of which sugars 3g; Fat 4g, of which saturates 1g; Cholesterol 0mg; Calcium 121mg; Fibre 1g; Sodium 385mg

1 Thoroughly rinse the skate in cold water. Bring a large pan of water to the boil and add the vinegar, peppercorns and thyme. Reduce the heat so that the water simmers.

2 Add the skate to the pan and poach it for 7–10 minutes, until the flesh is just beginning to come away from the bones. Do not overcook. Drain thoroughly. Remove the skate flesh from the bone with a fork, shred and set aside.

3 For the dressing, mix the grated pear, oil, vinegar, garlic, mustard and soy sauce. Season and mix well.

4 Place the rocket, watercress, mixed leaves and diced tomatoes in a large serving bowl. Add the shredded skate and toss the ingredients together. Pour the dressing over the salad, toss lightly and garnish with orange zest.

SPICED SARDINE SALAD   210 Calories

Oily fish are rich and nutritious, and more satisfying than white fish. Here the dense taste of sardines is teamed with fresh citrus and aniseed flavours.

8 fresh sardines, cleaned and
   gutted, 400g/14oz total weight
1 medium onion, grated
2.5ml/½ tsp ground cinnamon
5ml/1 tsp cumin seeds, roasted
   and ground
5ml/1 tsp coriander seeds, roasted
   and ground
2.5ml/½ tsp paprika
2.5ml/½ tsp ground black pepper
small bunch of fresh coriander
   (cilantro), chopped
coarse salt
1 lemon, cut into wedges, to serve

For the salad
1 small ruby grapefruit
5ml/1 tsp sea salt
1 fennel bulb
2–3 spring onions (scallions), finely
   sliced
2.5ml/½ tsp ground cumin
10ml/2 tsp olive oil
8 black olives, halved

Serves 4

NUTRITIONAL INFORMATION: Energy 210kcal/877.8kJ; Protein 23g; Carbohydrate 6g, of which sugars 5g; Fat 13g, of which saturates 3g; Cholesterol 0mg; Calcium 166mg; Fibre 2g; Sodium 620mg

1 Rinse the sardines and pat dry on kitchen paper, then rub inside and out with a little coarse salt. In a bowl, mix the grated onion with the cinnamon, ground roasted cumin and coriander, paprika and black pepper.

2 Make several slashes into the flesh of the sardines and smear the onion and spice mixture all over the fish, inside and out and into the gashes. Leave the sardines to stand for about 1 hour to allow the flavours of the spices to penetrate the flesh.

3 Meanwhile, prepare the salad. Peel the grapefruit with a knife, removing all the pith, and peel in neat strips down the outside of the fruit. Cut between the membranes to remove the segments of fruit intact. Cut each grapefruit segment in half, place in a bowl and sprinkle with salt.

4 Trim the fennel, cut it in half lengthways and slice finely. Add the fennel to the grapefruit with the spring onions, cumin and olive oil. Toss lightly, then garnish with the olives.

5 Preheat the grill (broiler) or barbecue. Cook the sardines for 3–4 minutes on each side, basting with any leftover marinade.

6 Sprinkle the sardines with fresh coriander and serve immediately, with lemon wedges for squeezing over and the refreshing grapefruit and fennel salad.

TOFU AND SPROUTED BEAN SALAD

132 Calories

This crisp and refreshing salad is ultra-quick to make and is bursting with the goodness of fresh shoots and vegetables, together with fragrant herbs and chilli.

55g/2oz bean thread noodles
250g/9oz mixed sprouted beans
2 spring onions (scallions), shredded
55g/2oz firm tofu, cubed
1 plum tomato, peeled, seeded and diced
¼ cucumber, peeled and diced
30ml/2 tbsp chopped fresh coriander (cilantro)
30ml/2 tbsp chopped fresh mint
30ml/2 tbsp rice vinegar
5ml/1 tsp sesame oil
2.5ml/½ tsp chilli oil
salt

Serves 4

NUTRITIONAL INFORMATION: Energy 132kcal/551.76kJ; Protein 8g; Carbohydrate 17g, of which sugars 4g; Fat 4g, of which saturates 1g; Cholesterol 0mg; Calcium 112mg; Fibre 3g; Sodium 202mg

1 Place the bean thread noodles in a bowl and pour over enough boiling water to cover. Leave to soak for 12–15 minutes, drain and refresh under cold, running water and drain again. Cut the noodles up with scissors and put into a bowl.

2 Fill a wok one-third full of boiling water and place over a high heat. Add the sprouted beans and blanch for 1 minute. Drain, transfer to the noodle bowl, and add the spring onions, tofu, tomato, cucumber and herbs.

3 Combine the rice vinegar, sesame and chilli oils and toss into the noodle mixture. Transfer to a serving dish and chill for 30 minutes before serving.

SMOKED AUBERGINE SALAD

132 Calories

Variations of this salad can be found throughout the eastern Mediterranean. It will keep well in the refrigerator. Non-fasting people can scoop it up with pitta bread.

500g/1lb 2oz aubergine (eggplant)
2 medium tomatoes, skinned, seeded and chopped
1 green (bell) pepper, chopped
1 red onion, finely chopped
bunch of flat leaf parsley, finely chopped
2 cloves garlic, crushed
30ml/2 tbsp olive oil
juice of 1 lemon
15ml/1 tbsp finely chopped walnuts
15ml/1 tbsp pomegranate seeds
sea salt and ground black pepper

Serves 6

NUTRITIONAL INFORMATION: Energy 132kcal/551.76kJ; Protein 4g; Carbohydrate 8g, of which sugars 7g; Fat 10g, of which saturates 1g; Cholesterol 0mg; Calcium 56mg; Fibre 4g; Sodium 178mg

1 Place the aubergines on a hot ridged griddle, or directly over a gas flame or a charcoal grill, and leave to char until soft, turning them from time to time. Hold by their stems under running cold water and peel off the charred skins, or slit open the skins and scoop out the flesh.

2 Squeeze out the excess water from the aubergine flesh then chop it to a pulp and place it in a bowl with the tomatoes, pepper, onion, parsley and garlic. Add the olive oil and lemon juice and toss thoroughly. Season to taste with salt and pepper, then stir in half the walnuts and pomegranate seeds.

3 Turn the salad into a serving dish and garnish with the remaining walnuts and pomegranate seeds.

CABBAGE SALAD

129 Calories

This low-calorie salad is full of tangy Thai flavours. It can be eaten on its own, or as an accompaniment to any type of grilled meat or fish.

15ml/1 tbsp vegetable oil
2 large red chillies, seeded and cut
  into thin strips
3 garlic cloves, thinly sliced
6 shallots, thinly sliced
400g/14oz white cabbage, shredded
30ml/2 tbsp chopped peanuts

For the dressing
15ml/1 tbsp Thai fish sauce
1 lime, grated and squeezed
60ml/2fl oz/¼ cup light coconut
  milk

Serves 4

NUTRITIONAL INFORMATION: Energy 129kcal/539.22kJ; Protein 6g; Carbohydrate 9g, of which sugars 7g; Fat 8g, of which saturates 1g; Cholesterol 0mg; Calcium 76mg; Fibre 4g; Sodium 168mg

1 Make the dressing by whisking the fish sauce, lime rind and juice and coconut milk in a bowl.

2 Heat the oil in a wok. Stir-fry the chillies, garlic and shallots over a medium heat for 3–4 minutes, until the shallots are brown and crisp. Remove with a slotted spoon and set aside.

3 Blanch the cabbage in lightly salted water for 2–3 minutes. Drain well and put into a bowl. Add the dressing to the warm cabbage and toss to mix. Transfer to a serving dish. Sprinkle with the fried shallots and peanuts, and serve immediately.

WHITE CABBAGE SLAW

51 Calories

Raw cabbage slaw in a lemony vinaigrette is a much healthier dish than one dressed with mayonnaise. This makes a delicious accompaniment to grilled chicken.

500g/1lb white cabbage
12 black olives
30ml/2 tbsp extra virgin olive oil
30ml/2 tbsp lemon juice
1 garlic clove, crushed
30ml/2 tbsp fresh parsley, chopped
salt

Serves 4

NUTRITIONAL INFORMATION: Energy 51kcal/213.18kJ; Protein 3g; Carbohydrate 5g, of which sugars 5g; Fat 2g, of which saturates Trace; Cholesterol 0mg; Calcium 87mg; Fibre 5g; Sodium 211mg

1 Cut the cabbage in quarters, discard the outer leaves and trim off any thick, hard stems as well as the hard base.

2 Lay each quarter in turn on its side and cut long, very thin slices until you reach the central core, which should be discarded. Place the shredded cabbage in a bowl. Stone (pit) the olives, if necessary, and stir them in to the cabbage.

3 Make the vinaigrette by whisking the olive oil, lemon juice, garlic, parsley and salt together in a bowl until well blended. Pour the dressing over the salad, and toss the cabbage and olives until everything is evenly coated before serving.

LEEK SALAD WITH ANCHOVIES

162 Calories

Chopped boiled eggs and cooked leeks are a classic combination in French-style salads. Extra flavour from the anchovies make this dish into a complete meal.

675g/1½lb thin or baby leeks, trimmed
2 eggs, hard-boiled
55g/2oz anchovy fillets in olive oil, drained
handful fresh parsley, chopped
a few black olives, stoned (pitted)

For the dressing
5ml/1 tsp Dijon mustard
15ml/1 tbsp tarragon vinegar
30ml/2 tbsp olive oil
1 small shallot, very finely chopped
salt and ground black pepper

Serves 4

NUTRITIONAL INFORMATION: Energy 162kcal/677.16kJ; Protein 9g; Carbohydrate 5g, of which sugars 4g; Fat 12g, of which saturates 2g; Cholesterol 104mg; Calcium 103mg; Fibre 4g; Sodium 679mg

1 Cook the leeks in boiling salted water for 3–4 minutes. Drain, plunge into cold water, then drain again. Squeeze out excess water, then pat dry. Shell and chop the eggs.

2 To make the dressing, whisk the mustard with the vinegar. Gradually whisk in the oil. Stir in the shallot, then season to taste with salt and pepper. Place the leeks in a serving dish. Pour most of the dressing over them and stir to mix. Leave for at least 1 hour.

3 Arrange the anchovies on the leeks, then scatter the chopped eggs and parsley over the top. To serve, drizzle with the remaining dressing, season and dot with a few olives.

WARM BEAN SALAD

219 Calories

Dried beans are great value both in cost and nutrition. This sustaining Mediterranean-style salad is delicious served as a main course, warm or chilled.

200g/7oz black-eyed beans (peas)
3 spring onions (scallions), sliced
a large handful of rocket (arugula)
30ml/2 tbsp chopped fresh dill
30ml/2 tbsp extra virgin olive oil
juice of 1 lemon
8 black olives
salt and ground black pepper
crispy lettuce leaves, to serve

Serves 4

NUTRITIONAL INFORMATION: Energy 219kcal/915.42kJ; Protein 12g; Carbohydrate 27g, of which sugars 2g; Fat 7g, of which saturates 1g; Cholesterol 0mg; Calcium 89mg; Fibre 5g; Sodium 382mg

1 Rinse and drain the beans, tip them into a pan and pour in cold water to cover. Bring to the boil and immediately strain. Put them back in the pan with fresh cold water to cover and add a pinch of salt – this will make their skins harder and stop them from disintegrating when they are cooked.

2 Bring the beans to the boil, then lower the heat slightly and cook them until they are soft but not mushy. They will take 20–30 minutes.

3 Drain the beans, reserving the cooking liquid. Tip the beans into a large salad bowl. Immediately add the remaining ingredients, including 75–90ml/5–6 tbsp of the reserved liquid, and mix well. Serve straightaway, or leave to cool slightly. Serve piled on the lettuce leaves.

BEETROOT AND ORANGE SALAD

84 Calories

The combination of sweet beetroot, zesty orange and warm cinnamon in this salad is both unusual and delicious. For picture, see page 135.

400g/14oz cooked beetroot (beets)
1 medium orange, peeled and
　sliced
30ml/2 tbsp orange flower water
5ml/1 tsp ground cinnamon
salt and ground black pepper

Serves 4

NUTRITIONAL INFORMATION: Energy 84kcal/351.12kJ; Protein 7g; Carbohydrate 10g, of which sugars 9g; Fat 2g, of which saturates Trace; Cholesterol 6mg; Calcium 36mg; Fibre 2g; Sodium 325mg

1 Quarter the cooked beetroot, then slice the quarters. Arrange the beetroot on a plate with the orange slices or toss them together in a bowl. Season with salt and pepper.

2 Gently heat the orange flower water, stir in the cinnamon and season to taste. Pour the mixture over the beetroot and orange salad and chill for at least 1 hour before serving.

GRILLED LEEK AND FENNEL SALAD

This can be eaten by itself, or as an accompaniment to some grilled or poached white fish. Select young or baby leeks, as they are sweet and tender.

450g/1lb leeks, trimmed and
    washed
1 large fennel bulb, trimmed and
    cut into wedges
45ml/3 tbsp extra virgin olive oil
2 shallots, chopped
100ml/3½fl oz/⅔ cup dry white
    wine or white vermouth
5ml/1 tsp fennel seeds, crushed
6 fresh thyme sprigs
2–3 bay leaves
good pinch of dried red chilli flakes
225g/8oz tomatoes, peeled, seeded
    and diced
salt and ground black pepper

Serves 4

NUTRITIONAL INFORMATION: Energy 145kcal/606.1kJ; Protein 3g; Carbohydrate 7g, of which sugars 6g; Fat 10g, of which saturates 2g; Cholesterol 0mg; Calcium 89mg; Fibre 5g; Sodium 210mg

1 Cook the leeks in boiling salted water for 4–5 minutes. Drain and cool, reserving the cooking liquid in the pan. Cut in half. Cook the fennel in the same water for 5 minutes, then drain.

2 Heat a ridged cast-iron griddle and cook the leeks and fennel until tinged deep brown, turning once. Place in a shallow dish.

3 Place the olive oil, shallots, white wine or vermouth, crushed fennel seeds, thyme, bay leaves and chilli flakes in a large pan and bring to the boil over a medium heat. Lower the heat and simmer for 10 minutes. Add the diced tomatoes and cook briskly for 5–8 minutes, until reduced and thickened.

4 Pour the dressing over the leeks and fennel, toss to mix and leave to cool. Serve at room temperature.

FRAGRANT MUSHROOMS ON LETTUCE   75 Calories

This quick and easy salad is served on lettuce leaf 'saucers' so it can be eaten with the fingers. Soft oyster mushrooms are perfect for this dish.

30ml/2 tbsp vegetable oil
2 garlic cloves, finely chopped
1 lemon grass stalk, finely chopped
2 kaffir lime leaves, rolled in
    cylinders and thinly sliced
200g/7oz/3 cups oyster or chestnut
    mushrooms, sliced
1 small fresh red chilli, seeded and
    finely chopped
juice of ½ lemon
30ml/2 tbsp soy sauce
2 Little Gem (Bibb) lettuces
small bunch of fresh mint, leaves
    removed from the stalks

Serves 4

NUTRITIONAL INFORMATION: Energy 75kcal/313.5kJ; Protein 2g; Carbohydrate 2g, of which sugars 2g; Fat 6g, of which saturates 1g; Cholesterol 0mg; Calcium 37mg; Fibre 1g; Sodium 562mg

1 Heat the oil in a wok or frying pan. Add the garlic and cook over a medium heat, stirring occasionally, until golden. Do not let it burn or it will taste bitter.

2 Increase the heat under the wok or pan and add the lemon grass, lime leaves and sliced mushrooms. Stir-fry for about 2 minutes. Add the chilli, lemon juice and soy sauce to the wok or pan. Toss the mixture over the heat to combine the ingredients together, then stir-fry for a further 2 minutes.

3 Separate the individual lettuce leaves and arrange on a large plate. Spoon a small amount of the mushroom mixture on to each leaf, top with a mint leaf and serve.

THAI ASPARAGUS

99 Calories

This is an excitingly different way of cooking low-calorie asparagus. Eat on its own or as an accompaniment to lightly steamed fish dressed with lemon juice and salt.

350g/12oz asparagus
30ml/2 tbsp vegetable oil
1 garlic clove, crushed
15ml/1 tbsp sesame seeds, toasted
2.5cm/1in piece fresh galangal,
    finely shredded
1 fresh red chilli, seeded and finely
    chopped
15ml/1 tbsp Thai fish sauce
15ml/1 tbsp light soy sauce
45ml/3 tbsp water
5ml/1 tsp sugar

Serves 4

NUTRITIONAL INFORMATION: Energy 99kcal/413.82kJ; Protein 3g; Carbohydrate 4g, of which sugars 3g; Fat 9g, of which saturates 1g; Cholesterol 0mg; Calcium 50mg; Fibre 2g; Sodium 333mg

1 Snap off the bottom section of the asparagus stalks and discard the woody parts of the stems.

2 Heat the oil in a wok and stir-fry the garlic, sesame seeds and galangal for 3–4 seconds, until the garlic is just beginning to turn golden.

3 Add the asparagus stalks and chilli, toss to mix, then add the fish sauce, soy sauce, water and sugar. Using two spoons, toss over the heat for a further 2 minutes, or until the asparagus just begins to soften and the liquid is reduced by half, and serve.

VEGETABLES

Eating plenty of fibre- and water-rich vegetables is always a help when counting calories, and the wonderful available array of textures and flavours adds essential variety that curbs monotony. Vegetables come from many parts of the plant – root, flower (cauliflower and broccoli), leaves (spinach or lettuce), seed (pulses) or fruit (tomatoes and aubergine (eggplant)). There is also good science behind eating as many different coloured vegetables as possible, as antioxidants collectively offer wider health benefits. This chapter includes accompaniments, but also dishes that include tofu, nuts or seeds for some complete meals.

◄ Spelt with vegetables and pancetta.
▼ Tomato bake.

BROWN BEANS WITH ONIONS & FETA

196 Calories

This staple peasant food is Egypt's national dish, known there as foul medames; it's a meal in itself, served with a leafy green salad with a spicy dressing.

175g/6oz/1 cup dried broad (fava) beans, soaked overnight
1 small red onion, halved and finely sliced with the grain
85g/3oz feta cheese, diced or crumbled
bunch of flat leaf parsley, roughly chopped
15ml/1 tbsp olive oil
2 cloves garlic, crushed
5ml/1 tsp cumin seeds, dry-roasted and crushed
juice of 1 lemon
sea salt and ground black pepper

Serves 6

NUTRITIONAL INFORMATION: Energy 196kcal/819kJ; Protein 15g; Carbohydrate 16g, of which sugars 4g; Fat 9g, of which saturates 4g; Cholesterol 15mg; Calcium 138mg; Fibre 12g; Sodium 313mg

1 Drain the soaked beans and place them in a deep pan filled with water. Bring the water to the boil, reduce the heat and simmer the beans for about 1 hour, until they are tender but not soft or mushy.

2 When the beans are almost cooked, prepare the red onions, cheese and parsley and pile each one into a small bowl. Drain the beans and, while still warm, transfer to a large serving bowl and add the olive oil, garlic and cumin. Squeeze in the lemon juice, season with salt and pepper and mix well.

3 Serve the warm beans with equal portions of the red onions, feta and parsley scattered over the top.

STEAMED VEGETABLES WITH A SPICY DIP 76 Calories

This Thai dish partners cooked vegetables with raw ones to create contrasting textures. Pea aubergines are sold in brine, if you can't find them use capers instead.

1 head broccoli, divided into florets
130g/4½oz/1 cup green beans
130g/4½oz asparagus, trimmed
½ head cauliflower, cut into florets
8 baby corn
120g/4oz sugar snap peas
salt

For the dip
1 fresh green chilli, seeded
4 garlic cloves, peeled
4 shallots, peeled
2 tomatoes, halved
5 pea aubergines (pea eggplant)
30ml/2 tbsp lemon juice
30ml/2 tbsp soy sauce

Serves 4

NUTRITIONAL INFORMATION: Energy 76kcal/318kJ; Protein 8g; Carbohydrate 9g, of which sugars 7g; Fat 1g, of which saturates Trace; Cholesterol 0mg; Calcium 89mg; Fibre 5g; Sodium 821mg

1 Place the broccoli, green beans, asparagus and cauliflower in a steamer and steam over boiling water for about 4 minutes, until just tender. Transfer them to a bowl and add the corn cobs and sugar snap peas. Season with salt. Toss to mix.

2 Make the dip. Preheat the grill (broiler). Wrap the chilli, garlic cloves, shallots, tomatoes and aubergines in a foil package. Grill (broil) for 10 minutes, until the vegetables have softened, turning the package over once or twice.

3 Unwrap the foil and tip its contents into a mortar or food processor. Add the lemon juice, soy sauce and plenty of salt. Pound with a pestle or process to a fairly liquid paste. Transfer to a serving bowl and serve surrounded by the vegetables.

PAK CHOI WITH LIME DRESSING

Heat from the chillies makes this a really fiery dish. Double up the helpings and eat on its own, or serve with a stir-fry for a complete fasting day evening meal.

10ml/2 tsp vegetable oil
3 fresh red chillies, cut into thin strips
4 garlic cloves, thinly sliced
6 spring onions (scallions), sliced diagonally
4 pak choi (bok choy), shredded
15ml/1 tbsp crushed peanuts

For the dressing
30ml/2 tbsp fresh lime juice
15ml/1 tbsp Thai fish sauce
125ml/4fl oz/½ cup light coconut milk

Serves 4

NUTRITIONAL INFORMATION: Energy 102kcal/426kJ; Protein 4g; Carbohydrate 6g, of which sugars 3g; Fat 7g, of which saturates 10g; Cholesterol 0mg; Calcium 14mg; Fibre 1g; Sodium 235mg

1 Make the dressing. Mix the lime juice and fish sauce in a bowl, then gradually whisk in the coconut milk until combined.

2 Heat the oil in a wok and stir-fry the chillies for 2–3 minutes, until crisp. Transfer to a plate. Add the garlic to the wok and stir-fry for 30–60 seconds, until golden. Transfer to the plate. Stir-fry the white parts of the spring onions for about 2–3 minutes, then add the green parts and stir-fry for 1 minute more. Transfer to the plate.

3 Bring a large pan of lightly salted water to the boil and add the pak choi. Stir twice, then drain immediately. Place the pak choi in a large bowl, add the dressing and toss to mix. Spoon into a large serving bowl and sprinkle with the crushed peanuts and the stir-fried chilli mixture. Serve warm or cold.

AROMATIC CHILLI-SPICED OKRA

194 Calories

Stir-fried okra with fresh grated coconut makes a great low-calorie supper that is quickly assembled. If you have some spare calories, serve with a poppadom.

30ml/2 tbsp sunflower oil
1 onion, finely chopped
15ml/1 tbsp mustard seeds
15ml/1 tbsp cumin seeds
2–3 dried red chillies
10–12 curry leaves
600g/1lb 6oz okra, cut diagonally
    into 1cm/½in lengths
2.5ml/½ tsp turmeric
90g/3½ oz freshly grated coconut
salt and ground black pepper
poppadoms, to serve, optional (1 x
    13g poppadom = 60kcal)

Serves 4

NUTRITIONAL INFORMATION: Energy 194kcal/811kJ; Protein 7g; Carbohydrate 9g, of which sugars 7g; Fat 17g, of which saturates 8g; Cholesterol 0mg; Calcium 310mg; Fibre 10g; Sodium 216mg

1 Heat the sunflower oil in a wok. When hot add the chopped onion and stir-fry over a medium heat for about 5 minutes until softened. Add the mustard seeds, cumin seeds, red chillies and curry leaves to the onions and stir-fry over a high heat for about 2 minutes.

2 Add the okra and turmeric to the wok and continue to stir-fry over a high heat for 3–4 minutes. Remove the wok from the heat, sprinkle over the coconut and season well with salt and ground black pepper. Serve immediately.

TOFU AND GREEN BEAN CURRY

129 Calories

This is a versatile recipe that you can add other types of vegetables to, depending what is in season. The tofu adds calcium and nutritious soya protein.

300ml/10fl oz/1¾ cups light
  coconut milk
10ml/2 tsp Thai red curry paste
30ml/2 tbsp Thai fish sauce
140g/5oz button (white)
  mushrooms
85g/3oz green beans, trimmed
140g/5oz firm tofu, cut into cubes
3 kaffir lime leaves, torn
1 red chilli, seeded and sliced
fresh coriander (cilantro) leaves, to
  garnish

Serves 4

NUTRITIONAL INFORMATION: Energy 129kcal/539kJ; Protein 6g; Carbohydrate 5g, of which sugars 3g; Fat 10g, of which saturates Trace; Cholesterol 0mg; Calcium 138mg; Fibre 1g; Sodium 351mg

1 Pour about one-third of the coconut milk into a wok or pan. Cook until it starts to separate and an oily sheen appears on the surface. Add the red curry paste and fish sauce to the coconut milk. Mix, then add the mushrooms. Stir and cook for 1 minute.

2 Stir in the remaining coconut milk. Bring back to the boil, then add the green beans and tofu cubes. Simmer gently for 4–5 minutes more.

3 Stir in the kaffir lime leaves and sliced red chilli. Spoon the curry into a serving dish, garnish with the coriander leaves and serve immediately.

MARINATED TOFU AND BROCCOLI

Tender tofu served with steamed broccoli makes a great low-calorie supper or lunch. If you have enough calories to spare, serve with a spinach salad.

500g/1¼lb firm tofu, cut into 4
   triangles
45ml/3 tbsp kecap manis
30ml/2 tbsp sweet chilli sauce
45ml/3 tbsp soy sauce
5ml/1 tsp sesame oil
5ml/1 tsp finely shredded ginger
400g/14oz tenderstem broccoli
45ml/3 tbsp roughly chopped fresh
   coriander (cilantro)
30ml/2 tbsp sesame seeds, toasted

Serves 4

NUTRITIONAL INFORMATION: Energy 213kcal/890kJ; Protein 18g; Carbohydrate 7g, of which sugars 5g; Fat 13g, of which saturates 2g; Cholesterol 0mg; Calcium 614mg; Fibre 4g; Sodium 1804mg

1 Place the tofu triangles in a heatproof dish. In a small bowl, combine the kecap manis, chilli sauce, soy sauce, sesame oil and ginger, then pour over the tofu. Leave the tofu to marinate for at least 30 minutes, turning occasionally.

2 Cook the broccoli in a steamer for 4–5 minutes, until just tender. Remove and keep warm. Place the dish of tofu in the steamer, cover and steam for 4–5 minutes.

3 Divide the broccoli onto warmed serving plates and top each one with a piece of tofu. Spoon over the marinade, then sprinkle over the coriander and sesame seeds and serve.

BAKED PEPPERS WITH PUY LENTILS

130 Calories

Low-calorie peppers develop a lovely sweet flavour when roasted or baked. Here they are teamed with sustaining Puy lentils and eggs, for a balanced meal.

75g/3oz/½ cup Puy lentils
2.5ml/½ tsp each of turmeric,
  ground coriander and paprika
2 eggs
2 (bell) peppers, halved and seeded
salt and black pepper

Serves 4

NUTRITIONAL INFORMATION: Energy 130kcal/543kJ; Protein 11g; Carbohydrate 10g, of which sugars 8g; Fat 5g, of which saturates 1g; Cholesterol 130mg; Calcium 60mg; Fibre 2g; Sodium 450mg

1 Put the lentils in a pan with the spices, 450ml/¾ pint/1 cup water, salt and pepper. Bring to the boil, and simmer for 30–40 minutes. If necessary, add more water during cooking.

2 Break the two eggs into the cooked lentils and stir through gently. Preheat the oven to 190°C/375°F/Gas 5. Place the peppers close together on a baking tray.

3 Fill the peppers with the lentil and egg mixture. Bake in the oven for 10 minutes until the egg white is just set. Serve hot with a green salad.

BAKED FENNEL WITH A CRUMB CRUST

96 Calories

Fennel is a very low-calorie vegetable that has a lovely aniseed flavour; it is often used as a salad ingredient, but is also delicious when baked, as here.

3 fennel bulbs, cut lengthways into
  quarters
30ml/2 tbsp olive oil
1 garlic clove, chopped
55g/2oz/1 cup day-old wholemeal
  (whole-wheat) breadcrumbs
30ml/2 tbsp chopped fresh flat leaf
  parsley
salt and ground black pepper

Serves 4

NUTRITIONAL INFORMATION: Energy 96kcal/401kJ; Protein 2g; Carbohydrate 8g, of which sugars 3g; Fat 7g, of which saturates 1g; Cholesterol 0mg; Calcium 54mg; Fibre 3g; Sodium 274mg

1 Cook the fennel in a pan of boiling salted water for 10 minutes or until just tender. Drain the fennel and place in a baking dish or roasting pan, then brush with half of the olive oil. Preheat the oven to 190°C/375°F/Gas 5.

2 In a small bowl, mix together the garlic, breadcrumbs and parsley with the rest of the oil. Sprinkle the mixture evenly over the fennel, then season well.

3 Bake for 30 minutes or until the fennel is tender and the breadcrumbs are crisp and golden, and serve hot.

SPELT WITH VEGETABLES AND PANCETTA   253 Calories

Also known as dinkel or hulled wheat, spelt is a nutty-flavoured grain. Serve this on its own, or on top of a slice of sourdough toast, which would add 63 calories.

140g/5oz/¾ cup ready-to-cook spelt
175g/6oz courgette (zucchini), sliced
85g/3oz green beans
140g/5oz/¾ cup canned cannellini beans
175g/6oz cabbage, shredded
1 medium carrot, sliced
85g/3oz sliced pancetta
2 whole garlic cloves, peeled
10ml/2 tsp extra virgin olive oil
1 dried red chilli, chopped
sea salt
toasted sourdough, to serve, optional

Serves 4

NUTRITIONAL INFORMATION: Energy 253kcal/1058kJ; Protein 11g; Carbohydrate 36g, of which sugars 5g; Fat 9g, of which saturates 3g; Cholesterol 15mg; Calcium 72mg; Fibre 6g; Sodium 557mg

1 Boil the spelt in plenty of lightly salted water for 50 minutes to 1 hour, until tender.

2 In a separate pan, with a small amount of salted water, cook the courgettes, green beans, cannellini beans, cabbage and carrot for about 5–10 minutes, until tender.

3 Drain both the cooked spelt and the cooked vegetables. In a large frying pan, fry the pancetta and garlic in the oil until the garlic is softened and the pancetta is crispy. Discard the garlic.

4 Add the spelt and all the vegetables to the frying pan. Mix well and season with salt and the dried red chilli. Fry for 5 minutes to heat through, then serve.

COURGETTE AND POTATO BAKE

150 Calories

This version of a Greek recipe reduces the amount of potatoes to bring the calories down. It's a good one-pot family supper, just serve larger portions to non-fasters.

675g/1½lb courgettes (zucchini)
225g/8oz potatoes, peeled and cut into chunks
1 large onion, finely sliced
3 garlic cloves, chopped
1 large red (bell) pepper, seeded and cubed
1 x 400g/14oz can chopped tomatoes
60ml/4 tbsp extra virgin olive oil
150ml/¼ pint/⅔ cup hot water
5ml/1 tsp dried oregano
45ml/3 tbsp chopped fresh flat leaf parsley
salt and ground black pepper

Serves 6

NUTRITIONAL INFORMATION: Energy 150kcal/627kJ; Protein 4g; Carbohydrate 14g, of which sugars 7g; Fat 9g, of which saturates 1g; Cholesterol 12mg; Calcium 58mg; Fibre 3g; Sodium 163mg

1 Preheat the oven to 190°C/375°F/Gas 5. Scrape the courgettes lightly under running water and then slice them into thin rounds. Put them in a large baking dish and add the potatoes, onion, garlic, red pepper and tomatoes. Mix well, then stir in the oil, hot water and oregano.

2 Spread the mixture evenly, then season with salt and pepper. Bake for 30 minutes, then stir in the parsley and a little more water, if needed.

3 Return the bake to the oven and cook for 25–30 minutes more, increasing the oven temperature to 200°C/400°F/Gas 6 for the final 10–15 minutes, so that the potatoes brown.

TOMATO BAKE

185 Calories

This is a great way of making the most of slightly unripe tomatoes, as baking brings out their flavour. Serve with a big green salad. For picture, see page 149.

15ml/1 tbsp olive oil, for greasing
800g/1lb 7oz ripe plum tomatoes, sliced
small bunch of parsley, leaves finely chopped
30ml/2 tbsp fresh breadcrumbs
30ml/2 tbsp grated Parmesan cheese
5ml/1 tsp ground paprika
2.5ml/½ tsp mild chilli powder
salt and ground black pepper

Serves 4

NUTRITIONAL INFORMATION: Energy 185kcal/773kJ; Protein 6g; Carbohydrate 29g, of which sugars 18g; Fat 6g, of which saturates 2g; Cholesterol 8mg; Calcium 137mg; Fibre 4g; Sodium 384mg

1 Preheat the oven to 180°C/350°F/Gas 4. Lightly oil a 40 x 50cm/16 x 20in baking tray or similar size dish, and arrange half the sliced tomatoes over the base, overlapping them slightly.

2 Sprinkle with some of the parsley, salt and pepper, and repeat with another layer of tomatoes, parsley and seasoning. Put the breadcrumbs, Parmesan, paprika and chilli in a bowl and mix together. Sprinkle over the top of the layered tomatoes. Bake for 45 minutes, or until golden brown. Serve hot.

COURGETTES WITH YOGURT GARLIC SAUCE

72 Calories

This simple recipe of grilled courgettes, served with yogurt and garlic sauce, is delicious served as a side dish with an omelette or slice of frittata.

5ml/1 tsp oil, for brushing
600g/1lb 3oz courgettes (zucchini)
125ml/4fl oz/½ cup thick natural (plain) yogurt
1 garlic clove, crushed
5 mint sprigs, leaves finely chopped
15ml/1 tbsp chopped walnuts
salt and ground black pepper

Serves 4

NUTRITIONAL INFORMATION: Energy 72kcal/301kJ; Protein 5g; Carbohydrate 6g, of which sugars 1g; Fat 3g, of which saturates 1g; Cholesterol 1mg; Calcium 101mg; Fibre 2g; Sodium 220mg

1 Cut the courgettes into slices on a slight diagonal. Heat a griddle or grill (broiler). Lay the courgettes in a single layer, brush lightly with oil and season with salt and pepper.

2 Grill (broil) the courgettes for 3–4 minutes on both sides until they are tender and golden brown.

3 To make the sauce, put the yogurt, garlic and mint in a bowl and mix well. Season to taste, and then add the walnuts. Serve the courgettes with the yogurt and garlic sauce.

INDEX